Virginia Fernández

Company

Robert H. Hacker

Billion Dollar Company

An entrepreneur's guide to business models
for high growth companies

LAP LAMBERT Academic Publishing

Impressum/Imprint (nur für Deutschland/ only for Germany)

Bibliografische Information der Deutschen Nationalbibliothek: Die Deutsche Nationalbibliothek verzeichnet diese Publikation in der Deutschen Nationalbibliografie; detaillierte bibliografische Daten sind im Internet über http://dnb.d-nb.de abrufbar.

Alle in diesem Buch genannten Marken und Produktnamen unterliegen warenzeichen-, marken- oder patentrechtlichem Schutz bzw. sind Warenzeichen oder eingetragene Warenzeichen der jeweiligen Inhaber. Die Wiedergabe von Marken, Produktnamen, Gebrauchsnamen, Handelsnamen, Warenbezeichnungen u.s.w. in diesem Werk berechtigt auch ohne besondere Kennzeichnung nicht zu der Annahme, dass solche Namen im Sinne der Warenzeichen- und Markenschutzgesetzgebung als frei zu betrachten wären und daher von jedermann benutzt werden dürften.

Coverbild: www.ingimage.com

Verlag: LAP LAMBERT Academic Publishing AG & Co. KG
Dudweiler Landstr. 99, 66123 Saarbrücken, Deutschland
Telefon +49 681 3720-310, Telefax +49 681 3720-3109
Email: info@lap-publishing.com

Herstellung in Deutschland:
Schaltungsdienst Lange o.H.G., Berlin
Books on Demand GmbH, Norderstedt
Reha GmbH, Saarbrücken
Amazon Distribution GmbH, Leipzig
ISBN: 978-3-8383-7331-7

Imprint (only for USA, GB)

Bibliographic information published by the Deutsche Nationalbibliothek: The Deutsche Nationalbibliothek lists this publication in the Deutsche Nationalbibliografie; detailed bibliographic data are available in the Internet at http://dnb.d-nb.de.

Any brand names and product names mentioned in this book are subject to trademark, brand or patent protection and are trademarks or registered trademarks of their respective holders. The use of brand names, product names, common names, trade names, product descriptions etc. even without a particular marking in this works is in no way to be construed to mean that such names may be regarded as unrestricted in respect of trademark and brand protection legislation and could thus be used by anyone.

Cover image: www.ingimage.com

Publisher: LAP LAMBERT Academic Publishing AG & Co. KG
Dudweiler Landstr. 99, 66123 Saarbrücken, Germany
Phone +49 681 3720-310, Fax +49 681 3720-3109
Email: info@lap-publishing.com

Printed in the U.S.A.
Printed in the U.K. by (see last page)
ISBN: 978-3-8383-7331-7

Billion Dollar Company

An entrepreneur's guide to business models for high growth companies

Robert H. Hacker

"When you can measure what you are speaking about, and express it in numbers, you know something about it; but when you cannot measure it, when you cannot express it in numbers, your knowledge is of a meager and unsatisfactory kind: it may be the beginning of knowledge, but you have scarcely, in your thoughts, advanced to the state of science"
- Lord Kelvin

Table of Contents

Foreword

Much is written about entrepreneurship, but little of it is of value to the aspiring entrepreneur. The "get rich" genre of books provides few valuable tools and academic books generally cover subjects of interest only to other academics. Perhaps the largest category of entrepreneurship books focuses on achieving self-employment. My view of the entrepreneur is not the self-employed owner/operator of the neighborhood dry cleaner. My view of the entrepreneur is the passionate, visionary company builder who does not yet know how big their company can be. This book is for the people who want to build big companies, say $100 million or more in annual revenue. Why is this my area of interest? Partly because I did it and partly because we need more Googles and fewer new dry cleaners. Two statistics perhaps provide clarification.

Five years after starting a business:

1. *98.3 percent of U.S. companies have annual sales of less than $5 million*

2. *3 in 10,000 companies have sales greater than $100 million*

This book is for the entrepreneur who wants to be in the second category[i].

In 1982 I was working in Japan doing strategy consulting for large Japanese multinationals such as Fujitsu and Marubeni. In the course of this work I met a young Indonesian entrepreneur, Hari Darmawan, who told me his business goal was "I want to build the Wal-Mart of Indonesia". Having become an authority on Japanese retailing, an industry that specialized in slow growth, the plans of this entrepreneur were very intriguing and so off to Indonesia I went. In 1990 we got serious about the plan and by 1997 the retail company we built had $1billion in annual revenue, was publicly traded and was larger than the next eight competitors in Indonesia combined. It is a rare and invaluable opportunity when one is involved in building a large company. Doing it in an emerging market like Indonesia makes the experience even richer.

Other credentials and background in entrepreneurship may be appropriate at this time.

1. *I have been an investor in four startups. Two failed, one succeeded (but not remarkably) and one company did a NASDAQ listing and became a U.S. market leader.*
2. *I have been in management of two venture-backed companies and managed four capital raises with VCs for early stage companies.*

In 2005 I began teaching at Florida International University and later became a Board member of the University's Eugenio Pino and Family Global Entrepreneurship Center then under the direction of Dr. Alan L. Carsrud. Working with the students on business plans and teaching entrepreneurship and business management helped me to refine my thoughts, especially in the area of bringing together academic theory and practical experience in a workable model for entrepreneurs. My intent here is not so much to make a contribution to the academic study of entrepreneurship but rather to provide guidance to entrepreneurs based on over 30 years of applying theory to practical applications in business.

The organization that planted the germ that spawned much of my thinking on both business concept and business model is Sequoia Capital, the world-renown venture capital firm in Silicon Valley. They may not recognize their influence on this book and all mistakes are only mine, but I wish to acknowledge that some of their writings started me down the road that resulted in this book. The Random Walks of George Polya by Dr. Gerald L. Alexanderson was also very helpful in developing a more profound understanding of heuristics.

Several people were helpful in getting this book written. My wife, Hortensia, has encouraged me for several years to write a book and share my business experience. Colleen Post and Jeff Stamp from Bold Thinking gave me the confidence to realize I had something to say that was original and helpful to entrepreneurs. Lastly, I should thank my students at FIU who forced me to continuously improve my ability to explain a "business model" through their questions, papers and constant looks of befuddlement in the early years of my teaching.

Miami, FL

June 2010

Preface

This book is devoted in part to a systematic approach to developing a business concept and to a greater degree to a formal process for creating a business model. To put these two themes in context, I first need to explain my view of a business and, in particular, how to build a large business. Business is a conflict between revenue growth and cash flow. In a properly managed business, one is always trading off revenue growth objectives and cash flow availability.

The constant effort to grow the business has many benefits, some of which are listed below:

- Growth tends to force one to constantly follow the customer and their changing needs and expectations
- Growth tends to produce economies of scale and lower unit costs
- Growth tends to force constant improvement in all areas of the business in terms of policies, procedures, operations and customer service (what the Japanese call *Kaizen*)
- Growth tends to be attractive to both early stage and public company investors, which may provide the capital to continue growth

All of these benefits, of course, cannot be achieved if the business runs out of cash. If the business runs out of cash, the business is dead. Therefore, any growth strategy has to be measured against the risk of running out of cash in the short term or before more cash can be raised. Cash flow, of course, is also the ultimate determinant of value in a business, which again creates a conflict with growth.

While profitability is obviously an objective, as long as the business has cash one really only needs to manage to achieve a future positive cash flow (or worse case a breakeven cash flow) before cash runs out. In other words, profitability is the third objective.

A startup company's objectives in order of priority are:

1. *Revenue growth*
2. *Positive cash flow*
3. *Profitability*

It is comparatively easy to manage margins to achieve profitability and much harder to attract customers and turn them into revenue.

The first three stages in the life of a business are shown below.

Stage	Revenue
1. Proof of Concept	0-$1 million
2. Commercialization	$1-3 million
3. Scaling the Business	$3-10 million

Proof of concept is the stage where you have a marketable product and one is madly running around looking for anybody who will buy the product. Commercialization is where you have identified a customer segment on which to focus but you still lack the proof that this segment has potential. Scaling the business is when you demonstrate that a large customer base can be served typically with positive cash flow results or even profitability.

Many businesses get stuck at revenue of less than $5 million, as the statistics in the Foreword showed, because they cannot manage the tradeoffs between revenue growth and cash flow or they prematurely focus on profitability. After demonstrating that a customer base exists in Stage 2, all effort should be focused on scaling the business (Stage 3), which is in large part executing on a growth strategy.

While I hope that my discussion of business concept and business model has some value to the reader, an equally important objective is to develop in the reader an attitude or a discipline in developing a business model using my formal methodology. The formal methodology is quantitative, but not advanced mathematics, and much of the discipline comes from reducing the thinking on business model to numbers. To paraphrase the quote from Lord Kelvin at the beginning of the book--if you cannot explain it in numbers, your knowledge is unsatisfactory. The elegance and simplicity of numbers also greatly facilitate understanding of the business model by investors. In fact, many sophisticated investors now read the financial model before the business plan because it is an easier way to understand the business model. A significant part of the discussion focuses on building self-explanatory models. Decision makers review this type of model (and do not need to delegate analysis to junior staff).

The discipline of reducing the business model to numbers has two other benefits, which are discussed in Chapter 4.

1. *The risks in the business model are easy to identify*
2. *The key performance indicators (KPI) for managing the business are identified*

The development of a business concept is perhaps the most misunderstood and challenging part of a startup. Inadequate course material at many universities is partly to blame. Web-based templates for a business plan also come in for part of the blame. Lastly, most people only develop one business concept in their lifetime and rarely take the time to write about the process. Simply put, a business concept must address four questions:

1. **What is the customer need?**
2. **What is the value proposition?**
3. **What is the differential or competitive advantage?**
4. **What is the size of the market opportunity?**

What separates my methodology for developing a business concept from most others is the heavy reliance on formally developing the business model (Step 4) and how it links to the financial model, which is what most of the remainder of this book is about. I teach a five-step process to develop a business concept, which also makes it easy to write a business plan, produce a financial model or prepare a PowerPoint for an investor.

The five steps are shown below.

The first three chapters of the book briefly deal with customer, hypothesis and industry analysis. I discuss them to set the stage for the discussion of business model and financial model, which are discussed in the next nine chapters. I conclude the book with a chapter on how to use the business model to manage the startup and the cash flow of the business.

Each chapter in the book concludes with real examples from Indonesia that illustrate the major theme of the chapter. One benefit from building a $1 billion company in seven years is the abundance of examples to illustrate concepts.

Chapter 1

Step 1 – Customer

Some pundits advocate beginning the development of a business concept by developing the product and testing it quickly in the market. This approach has one serious flaw. Capital, the scarce resource, is being used to provide the data for analysis. Why spend capital to develop data when research is so much cheaper. Therefore, I recommend starting the business development process by researching and understanding the customer.

Whether we refer to it as "customer need", "customer pain" or the "job" to be fulfilled (which may be Harvard Business School (HBS) current terminology), in all cases we are trying to understand the customer. We are not looking for just simple demographic information or customer research; we are also trying to profoundly understand the emotional or psychological background that explains the customer's buying behavior. As Garr Reynolds, designer and blogger (*Presentation Zen*), says "you have to empathize with the customer"[ii].

In fact designers provide some of the best guidance for how to understand the customer. Hartmut Esslinger, who amongst his many accomplishments did all of the design work for Apple in its early years and founded Frog Design, writes in his book, A *Fine Line*, extensively about understanding the customer as the basis for a product strategy. As stated in a Frog blog post, "really knowing their customers well – what motivates them, what they value, how and why they behave and buy what they do"[iii] is what companies need to understand to "connect" with their customers. Alberto Alessi, the third generation to run the famous, family-owned Alessi design firm devotes a good deal of an interview for the *McKinsey Quarterly* to the status value and social value of products[iv], which is his way of categorizing customer need. What all of these designers have is a systematic methodology to understand the customer, which they are then able to translate into product designs.

Many have said that the process of innovation is frequently more interesting than the result. At the risk of overdoing the techniques, three techniques that I recommend to understand the customer are Zaltman's metaphors, the Nintendo approach and the Abundance-Scarcity paradigm.

Gerald Zaltman is an emeritus marketing professor at HBS who believes that 70% of all human behavior is explained by seven metaphors[v], which are listed below.

	Metaphor	Concept	Example
1	Balance	Equilibrium	Starbucks
2	Transformation	Changing status	American Express Card Division
3	Journey	Life	University of Phoenix
4	Container	Keeping things in or out	LG refrigerators
5	Connection	Belonging or exclusion	Facebook
6	Resource	Survival	Federal Emergency Management

			Agency (FEMA)
7	Control	Order	TurboTax

By recognizing the metaphor that explains how the customer relates to the company's product or service one develops a richer understanding of the customer that shapes the product and the value proposition. What I have found from working with many early stage companies is that they do not have a profound understanding of their customer until they can explain them in terms of one of Zaltman's metaphors. For example, it is very complicated to explain why customers visit Starbucks. It's not the quality of the coffee or the price, it's not convenience but ambiance plays a part and it's not the beverage and food assortment. In other words, traditional retail or restaurant thinking does not explain the popularity. What does explain Starbucks is perhaps Zaltman's "balance" metaphor or the concept of equilibrium. Starbucks is our refuge from the hectic pace of daily life.

Another powerful part of this methodology is that when you think in terms of a metaphor to explain your customer, you should stick with the metaphor. Starbucks performance declined when they started to think of themselves as a coffee company in response to market share gains by McDonalds. If Starbucks had thought hard about how to increase the balance or equilibrium instead of expanding food, they might have continued to perform well. American Express is another example that may be easier to understand. American Express grew rapidly in the 1970s and 1980s because it exemplified the changing status or "transformation" of people (metaphor 2). Later AMEX bought a brokerage firm and a mutual fund company. Neither of these acquisitions was responsive to the changing status or transformation of Amex's customers and AMEX never achieved the synergies or economic benefits that were anticipated. When you have built up a strong "franchise" based on one metaphor, business development activities and acquisitions need to enhance the metaphor. **To diverge from the original metaphor is likely to be unsuccessful.**

If the Zaltman approach is too eclectic maybe Nintendo's approach is easier to understand. Rather than thinking of Sony and Microsoft as the competition, Nintendo thinks of their product as "something to do in a person's free time". Consequently, competition becomes very wide-ranging and not so traditionally defined. Nintendo's competition is reading a book, web surfing, jogging etc. With such a wide ranging view of competition, I think you are naturally led to define your product in terms of customer value and not fall into the trap of thinking only in terms of product features, technology and companies that compete with you. For example, if you compare playing Nintendo with reading a book, high resolution or screen refresh rates probably do not come into the conversation. Books have excellent resolution and no problems with refresh rates. Concepts of "challenge" and "multi-player" may be germane. Books do not provide a challenge to the reader and there is no competition involved. From these concepts we are on the road to understanding how Nintendo provides value to the customer. The Nintendo approach is a variation on understanding the job the customer wants to do. As the famous saying at HBS goes, "the customer is not buying a drill bit; he wants to make a hole". This broad-based but very simple understanding of the customer by how you frame the job (find the "hole") provides a clarity of understanding about the customer that simplifies customer need and additionally makes it easy to communicate throughout an organization. **Of course, the genius comes in defining the job or the need your product fulfills.**

The last technique I like is the Abundance-Scarcity paradigm, which has been discussed on the *Defrag* blog (perhaps amongst many possible sources). If you are looking for a new business idea, first look at what is abundant. Automobiles are everywhere in the U.S. so let us examine automobiles. Now let's look for the scarcity. Auto sales people have the lowest integrity rating of any profession in the U.S. according to several polls. People hate the process of negotiating to buy a car. The scarcity is an enjoyable, honest process to buy a car. Voila! CarMax! CarMax provides high quality used cars at a fixed price (no negotiating) and is the market leader in their industry. The customer experience at CarMax is much more than just "no negotiating" and the entire process reinforces an enjoyable, honest car purchase.

Google might be another example of Abundance-Scarcity. As the Web grew in the mid-1990s, information began to proliferate. First came better browsers (another example of the paradigm) and then came the early search engines such as Lycos and Yahoo. The scarcity that developed from the abundance of information on the web was the ability to find "what you want". Yahoo actually created the scarcity by sub-par search results and Google has temporarily satisfied the scarcity. However, in today's world information is growing probably logarithmically with the proliferation of social media. Once again businesses are responding to the scarcity of "finding what you want" through the hundreds of search startups and content aggregators, such as Calais, Evernote, and Wolfram Alpha, to cite just a few examples.

I consider understanding the customer profoundly to be the most challenging part of the entire five-step process. In summary, there is no simple foolproof way to understand customer need. I have given you some techniques or processes that may facilitate the discovery. None of these processes are easy to use, but if it were easy we would all have thriving multi-billion dollar businesses.

From a profound understanding of the customer, one then develops a product with the feature set to satisfy the customer need. I think this approach is more effective than developing the product and then searching for the market (customer). Great companies are customer facing, focused on the customer, and this approach should start as early as possible. I also think this approach tends to be more efficient because the initial capital is more likely to be used for customer acquisition rather than finding the customer.

Proof for the process of starting with the customer and then moving to product may come from the venture capital industry. Some of the most sophisticated investors are venture capitalists and many of these groups are focused on the huge opportunities in social media. To better understand social media many VCs have become bloggers. The VCs are not so much motivated by a desire to share the personal details of their lives, but rather by a desire to more fully experience social media as users or customers. They believe that their experience as customers will enable them to better identify opportunities, which are based on customer needs. If the VCs are starting with a focus on customer needs to better understand social media, perhaps we should all start with the customer.

Lessons Learned from Indonesia

In Indonesia we operated department stores similar to a J.C. Penney store under the name Matahari. The great thing about retailing is every day you get customer feedback through the sales of merchandise, assuming you have the appropriate management reporting systems. Of course, management reporting systems rarely tell you what products the customers want that are <u>not</u> in the store.

Over the twenty years I spent in Indonesia per capita income doubled from about $300 to $600. Also, during this time a middle class emerged for the first time and their needs had a profound effect on how we merchandised the stores. In fact, keeping up with these lifestyle changes was the biggest challenge. Two examples will illustrate this point.

In the early 1990s cable TV was introduced in Jakarta, the capital city of Indonesia. Overnight customers began coming into the stores and asking for the blouse they had seen on Madonna in an MTV video the night before. Historically, Matahari had been the fashion leader in Indonesia but we dictated the fashion. In other words we used "push" marketing and offered what we thought the customer should wear (and buy). With the advent of CATV, the market changed to a "pull" market where the customers bought what they wanted and not what we dictated they wear. This change from push to pull was a cataclysmic change in the market and it forced us to change the whole way we did product development. Now we had to offer the fashion colors from Paris and Milan each season, find suppliers who could copy the new designs from celebrities and learn how to sell accessories (which were an important part of a celebrity's wardrobe). By making changes in the way we did business to match the "new" customer we maintained our position as the fashion leader, which was the focus strategy of Michael Porter discussed in Chapter 3.

The second example about the customer and their changing needs relates to household goods—towels, furniture, counter top appliances, etc. As the middle class emerged in Indonesia, the first purchase was a car and the second was a home. In fact, I think anywhere in the world the emergence of a middle class is identified by the construction of housing at affordable prices. With these new homes, the owners wanted furnishings to make their homes look like the homes in foreign magazines. After we surveyed customers on what merchandise they wanted and we did not sell, we realized the emerging trend in household and responded. Turned out our lackluster household department had been growing at 30 percent for the last year and we did not know why until the survey.

I always tell my students that the first and most important part of business is to focus on the customer. In fact, I go so far as to say that every business decision should first be considered in the context of how it affects the customer. (Maybe certain accounting and finance decisions are the exception to the rule.) My near obsession with the customer was developed in Indonesia where the customer's lifestyle and needs changed dramatically over a twenty-year period.

Chapter 2

Step 2 – Hypothesis

At the conclusion of Step 1, the objective is to have sufficient understanding of the customer to have developed a tentative value proposition (defined below), which I have called the "hypothesis". Merriam-Webster defines hypothesis as "a tentative assumption made in order to draw out and test its logical or empirical consequences". The mistake that many new entrepreneurs make is that at this early stage they think they have a solution and not a hypothesis. The second most frequent mistake is that people complete all five steps in the process and think they have a solution--before going to market. The solution is actually a hypothesis until the company reaches at least $10 million in annual revenue. At $10 million you usually have proof that a product can be commercialized and that the business concept can scale. When the company is successfully scaling the hypothesis is transformed into a business because at that point the company has documented repeat customers, a proven method to acquire new customers or both methods to continue growing revenue. **Before $10 million in revenue treat your business concept as a hypothesis.** An example from business history may clarify.

Walt Disney, while an excellent example of determination, is perhaps a better example of an entrepreneur who constantly went back and changed his hypothesis until he established a sustainable business model. Over a twelve-year period from about 1920-1932 Disney faced constant problems with his hypothesis for an animation company. Characters, the stars of the animation, were lost in contract disputes, product distribution deals fell apart and the technology changed to "Technicolor". Almost all of the key parts of the original hypothesis proved wrong. Not until Mickey Mouse and the spin-off character Donald Duck appeared in Technicolor did Disney put together all the right assumptions to successfully serve the customer and establish a stable, sustainable business model. While Mickey gets most of the credit for Disney's success, I think Donald should get the credit for moving Disney from a hypothesis to a business because Donald provided the alternative content that doubled the revenue stream and more importantly made Disney animations more attractive for distribution. Successfully securing and sustaining distribution was the key factor in the growth of revenue and the transformation of Disney from hypothesis to a business.

A value proposition is the satisfaction of a customer need in return for an economic benefit to the provider of the product or service. The hypothesis for the value proposition is what one tests in Steps 3-5. Findings from each of these steps may send us back to Step 2 to reformulate the hypothesis or to Step 1 where we need to re-examine our understanding of the customer. Even if a problem arises in Step 5—Financial Model—it is better to go back to Step 1 or 2 and complete the process again rather than merely tweaking an assumption in the financial model. If tweaking an assumption were sufficient, Excel Solver would be a lot more popular. As shown in the Disney example, when the hypothesis does not work fundamental changes in the business concept or value proposition are required and "tweaking the model" is not sufficient.

Lessons Learned from Indonesia

Much as a business concept should be reduced to a single sentence, so should a value proposition. In the department store business in Indonesia the value proposition was four words—"fashion at popular prices". We sold fashion that our customers could afford to buy. Rather than the cheapest product in the market, we offered a quality and sense of fashion that matched our customer's pocketbook and aspirations.

Most people understand fashion when we talk about a Hugo Boss suit or a Gucci purse, but fashion should extend to every department in a department store. The success of the household department, discussed in the last chapter, was not just being the first to recognize the customer need but equally important in bringing in fashion merchandise. Plastic containers were in demand for leftovers, colored containers were even more popular and plastic containers in the latest colors from Milan sold out in days. A significant part of the success of Matahari was due to the fact that we brought fashion to every line of merchandise in the store. We understood our value proposition and the more comprehensively that we embraced it the more successful we got.

This same strategy is the reason that Target is the only retailer consistently successful in competing with Wal-Mart. Target brings fashion to every line of merchandise in the store and Wal-Mart focuses more on price.

Chapter 3

Step 3 – Industry Analysis

The purpose of the industry analysis is to develop the differential advantage for the business concept. Differential advantage or sustainable competitive advantage is the unique, sustainable factor(s) that preserve the value proposition and the operating margins despite changes in the competitive, technology, economic or regulatory environments.

Many entrepreneurs think of differential advantage simply as patented technology. If you have the capital to defend the patent, this may be one example of a differential advantage. Other examples would be product features, business process, business model, algorithms, merchandise assortment, joining together two technologies (e.g. robotic surgery), customer experience, product delivery, distribution agreements and many others.

Differential advantage is a key factor in establishing a barrier to entry for competitors. The difficulty of new companies to compete in the same space is a critical factor when venture capitalists select their investments. Low barriers to entry lead to multiple competitors, fights over market share and the resultant lower margins and profitability.

The industry analysis also provides the foundation for answering two important questions:

1. At what stage in the development of the market is the business concept (market timing)

2. How big is the market for the business concept

Market timing, the determination of the market's stage of development, is one of the most challenging parts of deciding whether to start a new business. Using the product life cycle curve, as shown below, as a proxy for a market's stages of development, the concern of the startup entrepreneur is in the tail at the left of the curve. Starting a business when the market or product life cycle is in the flat part of the curve at left (Stage 1) frequently leads to failure. At this stage there are few sales to be had, as shown below. Entering the market when the curve has the steepest slope (Stage 2) is the most attractive time to enter because there are many new customers to be shared by the competitors. Wait until the curve starts to level off (toward the right) and you need to take customers away from competitors (Stage 3), which is a more expensive process that leads to lower margins.

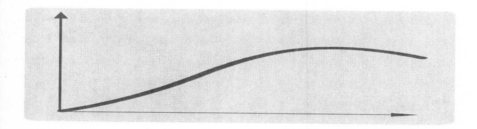

There are three scenarios for starting a new business:

1. Do something better (e.g. Google)
2. Do something in a new way (e.g. Amazon)
3. Do something new (e.g. penicillin)

In Scenarios 1 and 2 the market exists and is documented. Google could look at the results of Lycos and Yahoo and their comparatively high growth rates for revenue (Stage 2). Amazon could cite the performance of every bookseller but they had a higher risk than Google because the Internet sale of books had not been established (Stage 1). In the case of drug development or a new medical device, the customer need may be documented but there is little basis to determine whether the customer will buy the product or service. In terms of risk, Scenario 1 is the lowest and Scenario 3 is the highest. The risk that we are measuring is the market timing risk. Many business concepts fail because they are too early in a market cycle. Either the customer need is not sufficiently developed (there is no pain from the problem) or the customer cost to solve the problem does not create a compelling value proposition. An example may illustrate the point.

> For centuries business owners have wanted to know yesterday's sales results. For centuries businesses were successful without this information and sometimes waited months for results (e.g. Dutch East India Company). Not until the advent of more sophisticated programming tools, cheap Internet access and PCs did a market emerge for key performance indicator (KPI) reporting, business intelligence (BI) and enterprise resource planning (ERP) systems. Centuries of customer need and a viable business concept only emerged in the last twenty years.

How big is the market for a business concept is really a question that cannot be answered. I find that most professional investors such as venture capitalists and private equity firms actually ask "Is the market large enough to justify the investment requested? To answer that question, a little math makes clear one way to size a market, but I have placed it in Appendix A for the sake of readability.

Some may argue that the methods of investors to size a market may not be valid for the aspiring entrepreneur. To that I would say "hogwash". First, investors are constantly faced with determining market size as a key question in every investment whereas most entrepreneurs are assessing market size for the first time. Second, professional investors determine market size as part of the means to confirm expected return on investment and all entrepreneurs should have the same discipline of an expected economic return. Lastly, professional investors have return expectations that match the perceived risk of an investment (risk-return) and for an entrepreneur to develop a business model that would not satisfy a professional investor suggests a less than optimal business model. If the entrepreneur's required capital is small, such as in a web startup, perhaps the discipline of sizing the market can be relaxed. Of course this assumes that the entrepreneur can accurately forecast the capital required for his business plan, which in my experience is almost never the case.

In order to address the concerns explained above and develop a sustainable differential advantage, industry analysis is one of the most effective techniques. Fortunately, we can thank Michael Porter, Professor at Harvard Business School, for writing the definitive text on industry analysis. I always tell my students that there are only two business books that they need to read--Michael Porter's *Competitive Strategy* and Jim Collins' *Good to Great*. There are no significant concepts about business strategy that are not covered in these two books.

Porter's *Competitive Strategy* presents his model of the five forces that shape an industry. The five forces are:

1. ***Bargaining power of suppliers***
2. ***Bargaining power of customers***
3. ***Threat of new entrants***
4. ***Threat of substitutes***
5. ***Rivalry amongst competitors***

I am not going to rehash Porter's five forces, particularly considering all the good material available on the Internet and from Porter's Institute for Strategy and Competitiveness [vi] at Harvard. What are worth re-stating are Porter's three strategies for achieving what he calls "competitive advantage".

1. ***Cost leadership***
2. ***Differentiation***   + Access 2 capital
3. ***Focus***

Porter believes that these three strategies are the only way to generate sustainable superior economic returns. In other words, by these three strategies competition cannot take actions that force you to reduce margins and lower the economic returns.

Cost leadership is the position where you are the low cost producer through economies of scale, purchasing power or government granted mining concessions, to cite a few examples. Big box retailers such as Wal-Mart and Best Buy would be good examples of this strategy. Cost leadership should not be confused with price leadership, the lowest prices for the product. Price

24

leadership is never a sustainable advantage unless it is matched with cost leadership because the competition can always match a lower price not based on a cost advantage. The management focus is on lower costs according to Porter; pricing and gross margin become an option for management in this strategy.

Differentiation is the ability to develop products with unique attributes where the customer is willing to pay for the additional "value". Perhaps the best example of this strategy is the Apple MacBook or the iPhone. Never the low cost producer, Apple succeeds because they develop products with new features that the customer is willing to pay extra for. Inherent in Apple's success is their ability to provide a superior integration of software to a single device. Microsoft Windows, on the other hand, must work with as many as sixty different brands of computers, which rarely leads to Windows being optimized for a particular device.

Focus is the specialization strategy where you become the domain expert and focus on a more narrow market segment. Cisco, in its early years, would be a good example of the focus strategy. Cisco focused almost entirely on the internal data needs of large business customers and ignored telecom companies. Only later did they begin to offer products for carriers, when the growth in cell phones changed the demand for data. Focus was the strategy we used in Indonesia, where fashion at popular prices was the objective.

Porter's three strategies come from his grounding in theoretical microeconomics. Traditional microeconomics tends to neglect access to capital, which prompts my belief that there is a fourth strategy—access to capital. Capital is the scarce resource for most entrepreneurs. Just ask anybody developing a business in Guatemala, Botswana, Vietnam or any emerging market country. I believe that access to capital is a competitive advantage. If you are the only competitor in a market with access to capital or significantly greater amounts of capital, your company can grow faster, iterate faster and more easily achieve a position of cost leadership or differentiation. As may be obvious by now, any of the four strategies can be combined to enhance further the competitive advantage.

If you are reluctant to believe that access to capital is a sustainable competitive advantage, think about all the different financial products that can be used to raise capital. With some creativity, financing through these different financial products could go on for years, enabling a company to source greater amounts of capital at lower costs. An illustration from my time in Indonesia, a capital starved country, may illustrate.

In 1992 it was illegal for foreigners to own shares in privately held Indonesian retailers, which ostensibly meant that a venture capital firm could not invest in the equity of any retail company. By doing a convertible bond, instead of a common stock investment, we complied with the law and raised $20 million in capital. Eighteen months later the company became the first publicly traded retail company, raised additional capital and all the convertible bonds converted to common stock. With the caché of a publicly traded company, we then issued some of the first commercial paper in Indonesia (short term IOUs) and a year later did a $100 million 144A bond issue with Credit Suisse First Boston in the U.S. market. While the Asian Financial Crisis in 1997 put the end to further "firsts" in financing, at the time we were planning to do American Depository Receipts (ADR), which would have made us the first Indonesian retailer to list on a U.S. exchange. We were planning to follow the ADRs with U.S.

listed puts and calls on the common stock as a way to improve liquidity in the stock and raise additional capital. This capital raising strategy could have gone on, limited only by our imagination. Our competitors in Indonesia never raised the amounts of capital that we did and consequently we were the largest retailer in Asia outside Japan because of it (until the devaluations of 1997). While this is somewhat of an anecdotal argument I believe it illustrates how access to capital can be used to successfully grow a business faster than competitors in developing markets and achieve incomparable economies of scale in all parts of the business (IT, purchasing, distribution, etc.).

Note: leading academics such as Margaret Petraf and Jay Barney have advanced an alternative approach to Porter for sustainable competitive advantage. They call their concept Resource-Based Theory. In contrast with the external environment approach of Porter, Petraf and Barney advocate that internal social resources within a company, such as reputation, trust, friendship, teamwork and culture, can be woven together to create sustainable competitive advantage. An excellent paper on RBT is by Jay B. Barney *Looking Inside for Competitive Advantage* Academy of Management Executive, 1995 Vol. 9 No. 4. Although at times this may look like a book on corporate strategy, it is not. You will have to do your own research to better understand RBT.

Lessons Learned from Indonesia

As discussed above, I believe that access to capital can be developed into an alternative strategy to Porter's three choices. Greater amounts of capital allow a company to accelerate their growth to levels that the competition cannot reach. At times it may appear that you are driving a motorcycle across a high wire, but that is why we do financial planning (discussed in Chapters 11,12 and 13).

27

One of the most common mistakes I see is that entrepreneurs raise a large amount of capital before they have validated their business model. I believe that gradual capital raises are called for at least until annual revenues reach $30-40 million. At that point you can "bet the ranch" and go for a strategic differentiator amount of capital. At that point typically you should have a proven business model and equally important the management team to effectively use the capital.

While the growth stages are usually determined by annual revenue, a significant part of the transition from one stage to another is based on the development of the management team. In fact most companies that have reached a plateau in revenue are in the dilemma not because of market or competitive conditions but rather a failure to develop the proper management skills. As one plans for growth one must first consider the capital required, but the second most important topic is "do we have the management team and skills" to manage the growth.

Chapter 4

Step 4—Introduction to Business Model

A heuristic is defined as "the methods and rules of discovery and invention"[vii]. The power of heuristics is that they are a systematic step-by-step approach and they impose a discipline on the way one thinks about a problem. Many of the great thinkers in history have developed and applied heuristics to their areas of study. Leonardo da Vinci's work in first formulating the scientific method and George Polya's work on problem solving in advanced mathematics would be two noteworthy examples. Developing a business model is not as complex as advanced mathematics and does not require the intellect of Leonardo, although sometimes it may appear so. Hopefully the heuristic that follows will simplify the process of developing the business model. **To repeat for the third time, a significant part of the value in my way of thinking about business model is that it is a disciplined approach to the problem.** You may not enjoy the approach, but the discipline alone has value.

The Business Model, the fourth step in the process, explains how the growth in the business will be achieved. However, we should first clarify the difference between a productivity improvement and growth. If McDonald's extends the operating hours of a store, there is an increase in revenue (hopefully) but no additional capital is required. That is a productivity improvement. If McDonalds invests $5 million in capital to open two new stores, that is "growth" because the growth in revenue is directly linked to the deployment of capital. The business model explains how the growth will be achieved and identifies the significant uses of capital. The financial plan, Step 5, quantifies the capital required.

A business model has three parts:

1. **The revenue driver(s)**
2. **The pricing strategy**
3. **The sales and distribution strategy**
4. **The capital expenditure (CAPEX) plan**
5. **The headcount plan**

Parts 4 and 5 are optional. Part 4 is only required if CAPEX is a significant use of capital. With the same logic, a headcount plan is only required if the number of personnel is significant. For example, if the business model requires large call centers, a headcount plan would be useful to an investor to explain capital requirements.

In almost any business transaction, after defining the market opportunity, the next most logical question is how are you going to capture revenue from the opportunity and at what rate (growth). To answer these questions is a combination of three simpler questions:

1. **How is growth in revenue achieved, i.e. the growth driver**
2. **How will you price for the exchange of goods or services, i.e. the pricing strategy**
3. **How do you reach the customer to consummate the sale, i.e. the sales strategy**

One has to understand the answer to these three simple questions to understand most business deals and definitely a new business concept. So my concept of the business model provides a systematic way to answer each of the three questions, provides the possible answers for the first two questions (growth drivers and pricing) and forces you to systematically answer all three of these important questions.

Sophisticated investors also always understand the physical movement of goods or services (which includes things like a communications network) in a business so we include distribution with the sales strategy. If you cannot deliver the product or service to the customer you cannot close the sale.

Lessons Learned from Indonesia

The Merriam-Webster dictionary defines discipline as "orderly or prescribed conduct or pattern of behavior ". As an alternative to the popular notion that business is about "thinking out of the box", I have learned that discipline is a much better approach. The systematic application of rigorous analysis and basic theory in micro-economic, finance, statistics and operations research consistently helped me to make better decisions in Indonesia. Every pilot has a pre-flight checklist (the discipline) and these academic theories are the checklist for business. Everyone knows they should calculate the ROI of a new investment (the discipline), but microeconomics and operations research theory are equally compelling. Of course, the benefits of this discipline cannot be used if you cannot identify the theory to apply to the problem.

Sometimes the discussions surrounding a disciplined, systematic approach (the discipline) are as useful as the results of the theory. For example, the cost of cash registers becomes a significant expense when the store is 100,000 square feet (similar to the size of a Wal-Mart). The obvious question then becomes "how many cash registers do we need". Classic queuing theory (from operations research) tells us that a key determinant of the answer is "how long do you want the customer to wait in line?". My staff in Indonesia said to let the customer stand in line up to fifteen minutes to pay. I realized that such a disrespectful answer was indicative of a much bigger problem with customer service overall. We were looking down on our customers because they were comparatively poor and uneducated. Correcting that problem dwarfed in importance the question

31

about the number of cash registers, but I might not have discovered this problem without the systematic application of queuing theory.

Business is not as stressful as combat, but ask any soldier what got them through and they almost always answer "training". Actually, it is not the training, but rather the discipline to follow their training. My method of developing a business model provides a disciplined approach. Discipline is a fundamental concept in business (and many other parts of life) and using my methodology may   be   the   first   test   of   your   discipline.

Chapter 5

Business Model – Revenue Driver

The revenue driver (also called the growth driver) explains how the company will generate its growth in revenue or sales. Therefore, the revenue driver explains the critical concept of how the company is going to reach the customer to get the sale. By focusing on the means or method to interact with the customer, the business will be focused on growing revenues. There are actually only five revenue or growth drivers to explain how a company reaches its customer, which can be remembered by the acronym SANDS:

1. Subscribers
2. Accounts
3. New locations
4. Distribution
5. Sales people

Subscribers and sales people are typically the growth driver when the company is directly selling to the customer and location is not relevant to the selling process (as it is in retail). Accounts and distribution typically apply in B2B sales (business to business). New locations is the growth driver when multiple locations are required for the sales process. In a multi-location restaurant business, locations is the growth driver. In a single location, high volume restaurant business, subscribers is the growth driver. A note on the word "subscribers", a term that has confused my students for years. "Subscribers" is just a word to describe all situations where multiple, individual consumers are the customers and has nothing to do with CATV users or magazine subscriptions.

Subscribers or users are the revenue driver typically in technology businesses focused on the consumer, such as cellular, cable and websites. Subscribers are also the driver for consumer businesses based on real estate with a limited location, such as theme parks, hospitals and utilities. The growth in revenue comes directly from the increase in the number of users. When the revenue driver is subscribers, customer acquisition cost is a significant use of capital. The budget for customer acquisition and the assumption for the customer acquisition cost per subscriber determine the forecasted number of subscribers and drive the revenue growth. How to determine customer acquisition cost is discussed below.

Accounts is typically the revenue driver in B2B sales. If a company is selling sub-assemblies to industrial manufacturers, to generate revenue the key factor is account penetration--how many of the available accounts will become customers and at what rate. One may argue that a sales force is required to secure the sale and therefore the driver is sales people. If the sales people are order takers, "accounts" is the growth driver. If a sales person is required because of the complexity of the selling process, the length of the selling process or a financing component, then the growth driver would be sales people. However, if it is a team selling approach is involved with designers, spare parts, training, financing and sales, such as in selling airplanes to airlines, then the sales person is less important and the "account" becomes the most important factor to generate growth. **What is the most important factor to generate growth determines the growth driver.**

New locations are the revenue driver in real estate-based businesses where expanding the number of locations (hotels, restaurants, retail) is a larger growth driver than leveraging the location's revenue (utilities and hospitals). For example, McDonald's achieves a larger increase from opening one new store than anything it can do to improve sales performance at a single location. Therefore, the revenue driver for McDonald's is new locations. New locations also explain the growth driver in certain transportation businesses such as airlines and railroads. For these businesses to grow they need to add customer terminals in new cities, which is a form of real estate-based expansion.

Distribution is similar to the Accounts revenue driver but in distribution there is the leverage of multiple outlets. An example will illustrate the point. If you sell Wal-Mart a product, a supplier usually starts with one 500-store region. Expansion into other regions of Wal-Mart becomes the growth driver. This leverage (one account with 500 outlets) is what classifies the growth driver as distribution. Using distributors to sell your product is another example of the distribution growth driver.

Sales people are the principal growth driver in many service businesses, such as legal, accounting, consulting and enterprise software. In each case the seller has to be very knowledgeable about the product or service, must be able to adapt the product to the potential customer and serves as the principal contact between the seller and the buyer. Sales people are frequently combined with the accounts and distribution revenue drivers as a strategy, but the key factor is where the operating performance has to excel. For example, Kellogg's, the cereal company, operates a large sales force but the key objective is distribution through retail supermarket chains. Expanding this distribution network is the critical management task. In an enterprise software company the key task would be managing the effectiveness of the sales force because the customer is a one-time buyer. An example may illustrate.

Suppose we are operating a Class 1 web hosting facility that serves business customers. These large indestructible buildings host thousands of servers for client websites and applications and have direct connectivity to the Internet. The selling process is done through sales people typically. Is the growth driver in this business locations, accounts, sales people or maybe even subscribers? We could argue that a web hosting facility is like a utility so it should be subscribers, but establishing web hosting facility is a much more complex decision than choosing a phone service. The complexity of the customer decision suggests that a subscriber growth driver does not capture the real management task to grow the business. The same is true for locations. When location is the growth driver, tasks such as construction management, store location and demographic analysis are key management tasks. None of these factors are particularly important to the web hosting business. Accounts could be the growth driver because we are talking about a business to business relationship. However, I tend to opt for accounts when the number of business customers is rather limited and not as plentiful as in web hosting. That leaves us by default with a sales person growth driver, but that is not the only reason to choose this driver. Remember when I said that the customer had a complex decision to make in choosing a web-hosting provider. Whenever the customer decision is complex a sales person is usually required to close the sale. If a sales person is required to close the sale, the growth driver is sales people. If a sales person is required and the number of customers is large, sales people are the growth driver. If the number of customers is limited, accounts may be the growth driver because management should be focused on serving the account and the sales person becomes more of an order taker (which is what the sales people at Kellogg's are).

Sales people may also be the growth driver in a consumer sale where there is a complex value proposition, such as car buying, insurance and brokerage services. A chart that shows the growth drivers and their characteristics is shown below.

Growth Driver	Customer Characteristic	Example
Subscribers	Direct contact, simple sale, B2C	Telecom, utilities, hospitals, social media
Accounts	Simple B2B sale, team selling or repeat purchases	Industrial products, airplanes
New Locations	Greater sales increase from new location than productivity improvement	retail, restaurants, hotels
Distribution	One account provides multiple distribution points, B2B	Big box retailers, distributors
Sales People	Direct contact, complex sale	Professional services, enterprise software, consumer financial services

A technique I have found useful to check whether the growth driver is properly identified is to put aside your conclusion about the growth driver and instead think about the critical expertise the new business requires for success. If the expertise required does not match the growth driver, you probably have the growth driver identified incorrectly (or regrettably you have the driver correct and do not know what expertise is really required). For example, sales force management would hopefully be a key expertise in a management team with a business model using a sales force growth driver.

A list of industries and their typical growth driver is shown in Appendix B.

While identifying the growth driver is the first step, we are not done in merely identifying it. To fully understand the growth driver, we must outline the key assumptions that explain the growth driver and the related costs. The Merriam-Webster Dictionary defines an "assumption" as "a fact or statement taken for granted". The "facts" we present are numerical in form (numbers) and these assumptions (behind the growth driver) provide the numbers that demonstrate a profound understanding or lack thereof of the growth driver and the business. These numerical assumptions provide five additional types of information, as described below. The assumptions

1. *explain the risks in the business model[viii]*
2. *make clear industry knowledge*
3. *demonstrate business logic*
4. *make clear the key management competency that is required for the business to succeed*
5. *become the KPIs for the business*

If there is significant divergence from an assumption about the growth driver, there will be significant variation in the business cash flow, which is the risk we are most concerned about (because it may put us out of business). If an assumption is significantly different from industry norms, the entrepreneur's credibility is immediately suspect. If the entrepreneur chooses an unusual set of assumptions, their business logic (how they think about the business) is immediately in doubt. The key assumptions, those that have the greatest affect on forecasted cash flow, highlight where management competency is required and become the KPIs.

An example may illustrate.

Suppose we are developing a chain of fast service restaurants (which I do not recommend anybody do). The growth driver is new locations. Two key assumptions typically are number of daily customers and spend per customer at a location. To omit these two assumptions immediately leads to questions about management's business logic. Therefore, these two key assumptions should become the first two KPIs reported each day by location. If these two assumptions are wrong, the entire business concept is in peril, which highlights where the risks are in the business model. Also, it is very easy to check spend per customer against industry norms, which shows how assumptions demonstrate industry knowledge. Lastly, if we need to build new locations to grow the business, we need management competency or expertise in site location analysis (and construction management and menu development) in order to successfully predict daily customers.

The example below shows the assumptions for a company that uses a website to sell several software products, with credit card payment at download.

The growth driver is subscribers and customer acquisition cost explains how we are going to grow subscribers, which explains why the customer acquisition cost (CAC) budget for each of the first five years is detailed (A). Another key assumption is that of the people who download the software, 80% will become dormant users not interested in future products. Of the remaining active users, the sell through rate on future products is explained by product (B). The schedule for new product introductions is also shown (C). Many other explanatory assumptions about the growth driver are also included. For each of the five growth drivers, there are certain key assumptions about important costs linked to the driver. In this example with subscribers as the growth driver, customer acquisition cost is paramount (A).

Sales/CAC					
Customer Acquisition Cost	$	14.00	**A**		
Monthly Budget Year 1	$	20,000	Increase per month		
Yr 2 Monthly Budget	$	150,000	per month	Yr 4 Monthly Budget $	350,000
Yr 3 Monthly Budget	$	250,000	per month	Yr 5 Monthly Budget $	500,000
% Dormant Inactive		80.0%			

Products	Per Subscriber	Penetration %	Year Start	Gross Margin
Software	39.95	100%	**B** 1	80%
Upgrades		0%	0	0%
Sample Packs	49.95	15%	1	65%
Other Packs	79.95	5%	2	40%
Video Software	15.00	5%	3	40%
SAAS	5.00	5%	2	90%
The Producer	65.00	3%	4	60%

One of the questions that perplexes my students and many entrepreneurs is that they frequently identify multiple growth drivers in their business model or believe that over time there will be multiple growth drivers. **There should only be one growth driver in a business model** and that growth driver is the one where a change in an assumption has the greatest effect on cash flow. **In other words, the assumption change that has the greatest positive or negative impact on cash flow usually indicates what is the growth driver**. However, it should be noted that a business can evolve and the growth driver can change. For example, in the early stage of a medical device company, the growth driver is probably sales force but over time reagents, spare parts or supplies revenue could dwarf device sales. At the point at which after sale purchases is forecasted to exceed device sales, the company should probably change the growth driver to accounts and consequently change the management focus and add new KPIs.

For reasons that I cannot comprehend, many of my students think that the growth driver is the business model. Let me make clear, there are at least three parts to the business model and the growth driver is only one part.

Lessons Learned from Indonesia

In every successful business eventually the numbers become daunting. When sales are $40 million, a twenty percent annual increase is only $8 million. When sales are $500 million, the annual increase becomes $100 million. In Indonesia, if growth slowed below twenty percent, the stock price would have crashed. To maintain this growth rate at $500 million in annual revenue, all we had to do was open two million square feet of new retail space per year at an annual cost of $100 million and recruit and train six thousand new employees each year.

To successfully manage an enterprise of this scale, four planning assumptions related to revenue and capital expenditure were critical, which are listed below.

1. Number of new stores
2. Total new space (Sq. Ft)
3. First year sales per square foot (as a percentage of a mature store)
4. Capital expenditure for new store construction/square foot

The reader will note, for example, that if the capital expenditure/square foot is 10 percent over plan the total capital required increases by $10 million. The scale of this variance hopefully reinforces the theme that assumptions represent the risks in the business model and where management needs to have good discipline and KPIs.

Now, on to the second part of the business model—pricing strategy.

Chapter 6

Business Model – Pricing Strategy

The pricing strategy is perhaps the most neglected part of developing the business model. The pricing strategy basically answers the question "when we close the sale, how will we receive the revenue. Many pundits confuse the pricing model for the business model. An innovative pricing strategy such as freemium or BOGO is not a business model. The pricing strategy is only one component of the business model.

In the U.S. from the time we are little children we are taught that to buy something you pay in cash one time. In fact, there are at least 15 pricing models, as shown below. (A definition of each of the pricing models is included in Appendix C.)

Immediate	Deferred	Indirect
$/Unit	Free trials	Advertising
BOGO (Buy 1, Give One)	Freemium	Barter
Donations	Lease	
Rentals	Intervals (Time Share)	
Commissions	Service/Maintenance fees	
	Licensing (I.P.)	
	Additional services	
	Membership/subscription	

An example of the power of the pricing model may illustrate the point.

For more than 80 years cute little girls have gone door-to-door selling delicious Girl Scout cookies once a year. If the Girl Scouts thought about their pricing model, the question I would ask is why they do not sell annual subscriptions to the cookies. Pay once and have the cookies delivered every month throughout the year. The number of customers might decline but the revenue per customer would increase and I think the total revenue would increase for the Girl Scouts. If 1,000 customers buy a single box of cookies at $6, then only 84 customers have to buy the annual subscription ($72) to breakeven in revenue terms.

This is the power that may be available to the entrepreneur from methodically thinking through the pricing model. (An additional benefit to the Girl Scouts would be that Wal-Mart's recently announced knock off Girl Scout cookies would probably take away fewer customers because subscription customers are stickier.)

Pricing models explain the critical question of when and how a product or service is paid for. Much of the thinking about business models has developed as a result of the proliferation of social media and Web 2.0. One of the more challenging questions in analyzing these new types of companies is determining the pricing strategy and much of the new thinking on pricing strategies in recent years has come from this sector.

Pricing strategies fall into three categories:

1. *Immediate (payment)*
2. *Deferred*
3. *Indirect*

With immediate pricing strategies, the cash for the product or service is received immediately or even prepaid. In deferred pricing models, the payment is either deferred over time or the event that generates the revenue is in the future. The indirect pricing model is used where the revenue is derived from a source not related to the revenue driver. For example, at Google the revenue driver is subscribers, but the subscribers typically do not pay for the service. The same situation exists in barter. The number of trades does not generate the revenue but rather when a trade is ultimately sold for cash.

Many may take exception to the categories for pricing strategies or the various examples of each. The important point for the entrepreneur to remember is that pricing strategy provides a means to differentiate your product and achieve a competitive advantage—if you don't skip over pricing strategy. The pricing strategy is also a critical component of determining the value proposition for the customer.

Lessons Learned From Indonesia

Indonesia did not afford me many examples to illustrate pricing models. However, when we started to accept credit cards in the stores we got an annual increase in sales of twenty percent and the average transaction on a credit card was 400 percent higher than a cash sale. Strictly speaking, probably not an example of pricing strategy, but I think it illustrates the power of consciously thinking about the pricing strategy and the effect it might have on customer behavior.

Chapter 7

Business Model – Sales and Distribution Strategy

Sales, simply defined, is the identification, pitching and closing of the customer. Distribution is the physical movement of goods to satisfy the sales transaction. Sales and distribution are not taught in most undergraduate and graduate business schools. In fact, a reliable source tells me that only one university in the U.S. grants a BA degree in sales. Distribution may be gaining popularity through logistics courses, but these courses tend to focus on supply chain management rather than to be customer focused. Many business plans I see are unworkable because of insufficient attention to sales and distribution strategy. An example may illustrate the point.

> The company's objective is to facilitate the sale of used textbooks between university students through a slick website. To deliver the books and collect the payment the students will meet face to face and the website will offer a meeting scheduler. Scheduling the meeting generates a commission for the company. The problem is that no college age woman will meet a male stranger, especially when she is known to be carrying $80 to pay for a textbook (at least at any university in a major city). Problems with physical delivery of the books (distribution) make this business concept unworkable as formulated.

Sales strategy is perhaps best understood by looking at two popular sales examples—direct sales force and websites. With a sales force, the questions that need to be answered (the assumptions) to describe the strategy are:

- How many prospects are there
- How will the prospects be reached (direct calling, tradeshows, web inquiries, etc.)
- How will prospects be qualified
- What are the attrition rates at the various stages in the sales funnel
- How long is the sales cycle
- What is the average revenue per customer
- What is the probability of repeat sales or add-on sales
- What sales support is required (brochures, videos, WEBEX, trainers, etc.)

In the case of websites, I define the sales strategy in terms of customer acquisition cost. The selling strategy becomes effectively managing the acquisition of customers at the budgeted customer acquisition cost. Customer acquisition cost is determined by valuing a customer over their expected life (as a customer) and then taking a percentage of this value as the customer acquisition cost. An example may illustrate.

A phone company typically loses their customer after 18 months. Monthly revenue per customer is $40 and gross margin is 50 percent. Assuming no marginal SG&A cost per customer, the value of the customer is $360 (18 x 40 x .50). Given the relatively short life of the customer $60 for customer acquisition cost or three months gross margin contribution may be appropriate.

What I have found is that similar companies in the same industry use similar customer acquisition cost assumptions. Therefore, by talking to people in your industry, you can develop valuable information about customer life, value of a customer and customer acquisition cost to consider using in your business model and financial plan.

4

I think customer acquisition cost is a powerful tool and I calculate it regardless of the business model. One of the most helpful uses is in determining sales force compensation schemes. All of the costs of a sales person are part of customer acquisition cost. After you calculate lifetime value of the customer and the customer acquisition cost, you then face the challenge of allocating the customer acquisition budget to marketing, advertising, sales force, etc. When I make such an allocation I first determine how much money goes to compensate and motivate the sales force (if the sales force is the growth driver) and then I look at how reasonable is the expected amount of cash left to cover mushy stuff like marketing and advertising, if any.

Distribution strategy, the physical movement of goods, is a key factor in developing a business model, especially when pursuing Porter's cost leadership strategy. Just ask Wal-Mart, McDonald's and Amazon. I might argue that Wal-Mart's excellence in physical distribution is the heart of their low cost strategy. Jeff Bezos' insight to have the book distributors fulfill the orders at Amazon was a key part of the business model, which freed up capital from inventory to accelerate the growth of the business. Much as careful thinking about pricing strategy provides an opportunity to create a differential advantage, distribution strategy provides the same opportunity.

Lessons Learned From Indonesia

The following story illustrates the power of thinking about distribution strategy. In the early days in Indonesia the checkout procedure was designed to reduce customer theft. (In fact, we lost a lot more money from employee theft and

47

accounting errors, but that is another story.) If a shopper wanted to purchase merchandise, first they went to a counter, surrendered their merchandise and received a paper, numbered receipt. Then they took the receipt to the cashier, paid for the merchandise, had their paper receipt stamped and then returned to the first counter where they surrendered the stamped receipt and picked up their merchandise. Elapsed time ten minutes, except on busy days when it might take twenty minutes to make a purchase. After discussing for several months a change in this procedure to a simple American or European checkout procedure, the owner of the company finally agreed to make the change. After a few months of testing, an executive announced at a staff meeting that shrinkage had "doubled" from one to two percent. The owner went ballistic...until I explained that we had gotten a twenty two percent increase in sales after the change (and the positive effect on sales normalized at eighteen percent). At a thirty percent gross margin, the sales increase easily covered the increased loss from shrinkage.

Note: I said this story illustrates distribution strategy—how the customer physically receives the product. In considering distribution strategy, the analysis is not finished until the product or service is in the customer's hands.

I have a funny story about cash registers. When investors did the due diligence on a bond issue by Matahari, one investor asked me if we had cash registers in the stores. I resisted the urge to answer "we use cigar boxes" and politely answered that we had cash registers in all our stores. In fact, the cash registers were linked to head office by satellite to facilitate daily polling of point-of-sale information (POS). I believe we were the second retailer in Asia after Daiei in Japan to poll POS information through a satellite-based network. Point of the story...always be polite to investors even when they ask really dumb questions. Despite a widely held belief that all Moslem countries have camels, Indonesia does not have a single camel except perhaps in a zoo. I was very tempted to show this investor the camel parking area at a store, but I refrained. FYI—it's next to the elephant parking ☺

Chapter 8

Business Model—Capital Expenditure (CAPEX)

The capital expenditure plan is required in the business model only if CAPEX is a significant use of capital (say more than 20 percent of the capital required). For any business where the growth driver is locations, a CAPEX plan would be useful and critical to understand the economics of the business model. Another example might be a web-based business where the IT infrastructure requires investment to scale in order to add servers, data storage, etc. A third example would be in most telecom businesses that involve a voice, data or voice and data network. Here the CAPEX plan would not only clarify the capital required but would also make clear the particular technology being used.

The objective of the CAPEX plan is to demonstrate when additional CAPEX is required. Increases can be linked, for example,, to subscribers and physical capacity (telecom switches, data storage), staff additions (call centers) and new locations (e.g. restaurants, stores).

An important point in developing the CAPEX plan is to document "unit economics", the return associated with additional capital expenditure. I am not asking for the economics of every new piece of equipment in a business model, but I would expect to see clearly the returns from additional investment in capacity constrained equipment that is directly related to revenue or for a new operating location (stores, restaurants, hotels).

Many people build models where unit economics are hard to determine. Every business model should easily demonstrate unit economics and related return on investment (ROI). The simplest way to do this, for example in a retail company, is to model each store individually on a separate tab or create a separate tab that shows the investment and expected cash flows for a model store. In a telecom company or website-based business, one would calculate the marginal contribution from the new investment in major pieces of new equipment that generate revenue, such as servers.

As a general guideline, the ROI on a marginal investment in CAPEX should probably exceed 25 percent. While this is an arbitrary assumption, it provides plenty of margin for the uncertainties of early stage companies or emerging market conditions.

An illustration of the assumptions for CAPEX in a "triple play" (voice, data, CATV) telecom company is shown below.

In looking at this example we see that one of the significant capital expenditures is for a Voice CMTS (highlighted) and that we need to add a new CMTS for every 40,000 subscribers (highlighted). Therefore, when subscribers surpass 40,000 we have a significant capital expenditure. Therefore, we would calculate the marginal contribution (marginal revenues less marginal costs) from voice for the customers from 40,001-80,000 for each period and then discount it back to determine the ROI. We would do a similar calculation for every significant capital expenditure such as the voice mail server or the soft switch, where capacity constraints exist and the number of subscribers will force additional expenditure.

Assumptions

Cable Service
ARPU	$14,50
% Attrition	3%
Customer Acquisition Cost	$5.00
Installation Fee	na

Data Service
% with Data	35%
ARPU	$40.00
% Attrition	1%
Customer Acquisition Cost	$5.00

Voice Service
% with Voice & Data	20%
% with Voice	25%
ARPU Voice	$20.00
ARPU Voice/Data	$50.00
Attrition	0.03
Customer Acquisition cost	$10.00
Existing Subscribers	0

Voice Minutes Subscriber/Month
Total Call Minutes per Month	400.00
Subs Roaming Other Networks Minutes	0.00
Subs-International Minutes	40.00
Subs-Terminating Off Net Minutes	320.00
Subs-Terminating On Net Minutes	40.00

Voice Revenue/Minute

Subs Roaming Other Networks	$0.00
Subs-International Calls	$0.10

Voice Minute Costs

Local Termination-Off Net	$0.02
International Calls	$0.01
Roaming Other Net	$0.02
Local Termination-On Net	na

Termination Revenue Non-subscribers

Minutes/Subscriber	5
Increase per Year	20%
Revenue/Minute	$0.02

Cable Content

Cost per Subscriber	$15
Annual Reduction Starting Year 2	20%

Trunks

Data Subscribers/Trunk E-1	10,000
Voice subscribers/Trunk E-1	5,000
Carrier Interconnections Voice	4
Cost per Data Trunk	$1,500
Cost per Voice Trunk	$1,500

CAPEX

Voice CMTS Initial Cost	$250,000
CMTS Cost Per Subscriber	$20.00
CMTS Initial Capacity Subs	4,000
CMTS Max Capacity Subs	40,000
Soft Switch Initial Payment	$75.000
Soft Switch Cost Per Subscriber	$80

Soft Switch Maintenance per Year	$200,000
Voice Mail Server	$200,000
Voice Provisioning System	$200,000
Edge Router/Subs	1,000
Edge Router Cost	$10,000
Core Routers	2
Core Router Cost	$25,000

Customer Premise Equipment

CPE-Cable Modem	$50.00
CPE-Voice Adaptor	$25.00
CPE-Router	$25.00

CAPEX Headend

Voicemail	$200,000
Provisioning	$200,000
Miscellaneous Equipment	$200,000
Ethernet Radios	na
Billing system	$300,000
Telecom License	$2,000,000
Miscellaneous Costs	$1,000,000

Subscriber Construction Cost

Penetration per Households	35%
Cost per Household	$55.00
Cost to individual Home	$40.00

Long Run Fiber

Long fiber	$92,000
Miles	50
Start date	2/1/13

2 Way Fiber/RF Cost	
2 Way FIBER/RF Upgrade Cost Per Mile	$4,000
2 Way Miles per Subscriber	0.01
Depreciation Life Months	60
Advertising Revenue per Sub	$1.00

Lessons Learned From Indonesia

While new store build out was the single largest CAPEX every year at Matahari, every year we also invested a significant amount in IT, software, networking, etc. We had the best IT department in the country as evidenced by the fact that everybody tried, unsuccessfully, to recruit away the IT executives. No one ever left because we were doing the most interesting projects every year and that is what attracts good IT executives and programmers.

In all the years that I oversaw the IT at Matahari, I never once did an ROI calculation on an IT investment. My logic was that superior information to the competitors was an incredible advantage in shaping the customer experience and merchandising the stores. As long as my IT investment was customer directed, such as POS, I did not believe that an ROI calculation was warranted. Good decisions about the customer rarely produce bad investment decisions.

Chapter 9

Business Model--Headcount Plan

If a significant amount of capital is being devoted to headcount additions, there should be a schedule that details the title of the position, the annual salary and the start date. If additions to staff are based on revenue or customer growth, a formula linked to revenue or customer count would be substituted for start date. Benefits, payroll taxes and bonuses are also included by individual or as a group.

Headcount plans are particularly important in demonstrating industry knowledge and business logic. Based on industry there are standards for compensation for many positions and especially sales people. Therefore, one would expect to see similar plans and costs in your startup business plan. Too low a compensation scheme and no good sales people will join the new company. Too high a compensation scheme and every investor will ask "why". Equally informative in the headcount plan is the rollout plan for staff additions. If you start a new company with five people and three are sales people, you send a strong message about the sales priority. Start the same five-person company and recruit a CEO, CMO (chief marketing officer), CFO, controller and a receptionist and there is a lot of overhead but not much apparent concern about sales. **Every part of the business model demonstrates industry knowledge and business logic. Make sure you know what story you are telling!** Early stage companies should predominantly invest in sales and product development people (designers, programmers, engineers). The smallest amount possible should be spent on other positions, except for perhaps a qualified controller (when sales start to materialize).

Two examples of headcount plans follow. The first example shows a start date driven plan. The next example illustrates the detail required in a business model where the growth driver is sales people. All of this detail is captured in part to make it easier to determine customer acquisition cost.

Running Month			1	2	3	4	5
Employee Headcount	Start Month	Salary					
Engineering							
CTO	1	130,000	10,833	10,833	10,833	10,833	10,833
Software Manager	1	115,000	9,583	9,583	9,583	9,583	9,583
Mechanical Design M	1	100,000	8,333	8,333	8,333	8,333	8,333
Regulatory							
RA/QA Director	1	125,000	10,417	10,417	10,417	10,417	10,417
Clinical Training Mgr	3	90,000	.	.	7,500	7,500	7,500
Technical Writer	5	80,000	.	.	.	.	6,667

Salesperson Compensation
    Base salary
    Incentive compensation
    Standard commissions
    Residual commissions
        Total

Salesperson Related Expenses
    Recruiting fees
    Benefits
    Travel & Entertainment
    Car
    Phone
        Total

Lessons Learned From Indonesia

Headcount planning is a critical annual exercise in any labor-intensive business, such as retail, hotels or call centers. There is a tendency, however, not to consider this planning on a multi-year basis. For example, in Indonesia we needed twenty new store managers every year. Each mature store averaged

$10 million in annual sales and being the store manager was a high status position in the community. Our analysis showed that it took three years to develop a properly trained manager. We always promoted from within, so at any given time we were tracking the performance and promotion potential of 100-150 junior store staff that we believed had the potential to become store managers. Tracking staff to insure the necessary number of new managers was complicated by the fact that Indonesians do not typically relocate within Indonesia. We had to maintain an adequate pool of manager candidates for each city or region on a multi-year basis. The ability to manage this manager development process was a critical factor in the success of Matahari and it all began with a systematic approach to headcount planning.

Chapter 10

Final Thoughts on Business Model

There are three key parts to develop the business model and two optional parts. Together these concepts make clear how the company will execute the critical parts of the business concept. The discipline in following each of the steps ensures that a founder will not overlook a critical area of the business. Additionally, the discipline of choosing one of the five growth drivers forces the founder to distill his growth strategy down to a single approach. **If you cannot identify the single growth driver from the five choices, you have not sufficiently thought about your business** (and therein lies the discipline my method provides). As the earlier web-hosting example made clear, it is not always easy to select the appropriate growth driver. How the sale is consummated or the nature of the selling process typically highlights the correct growth driver. Also, similar businesses in the same industry have the same growth driver. Lastly, remember that the critical management expertise in the business is directly associated with the growth driver. Systematically thinking about pricing, sales strategy and distribution further define the business concept.

In developing each of the five parts of the business model, assumptions should be developed that clearly explain how a growth driver or strategy in the model works. These assumptions serve four purposes:

- They demonstrate your business logic (how you think about and will operate the business)
- They demonstrate your industry knowledge
- They demonstrate the risks in the model or plan

- They serve as the basis for the first part of Step 5--the financial model.

Early stage entrepreneurs should scrutinize the assumptions and consider them in each of the four ways described above.

I have come to the conclusion that we over complicate the teaching of business management in the U.S. To effectively run a business, management has three important tasks:

1. Focus on the customer
2. Manage the growth driver in the business
3. Manage cash flow

Now we turn to building the financial model. The financial model gives us the in-depth understanding of cash flow and capital requirements.

Note: The discussion in this book is by no means complete in terms of managing these critical tasks. I am also assuming that to manage the three critical tasks one needs a good team that is treated fairly, motivated and compensated properly (human resources management), but all of this was covered in the Ten Commandments, the Koran and the Talmud to name just a few good sources on human resources management.

Lessons Learned From Indonesia

To successfully grow a large company an entrepreneur requires two abilities-- discipline and focus. I have already discussed discipline, but the importance of focus is equally critical. Many entrepreneurs hit a sales plateau somewhere between $3 million and $10 million. Many mistakenly then diversify into a new business or a new customer segment. The error in this approach is that all of the skills and market knowledge from the first business rarely transfer from the original business. These entrepreneurs effectively are beginning a new startup with all of the associated risks.

In Indonesia many foreign retailers approached us to partner for the launch of their successful retail concepts. I consistently turned down these offers, even though some of these businesses could have easily grown to $100 million in annual sales. We were still learning how to run a department store business and could not afford the management distraction of starting a new business. Also, department store skills do not easily transfer to other retail formats. As McKinsey the prestigious consulting firm says, "stick to your knitting".

The one time that I lost the argument over a new business was when we added supermarkets to our stores. This move was prompted by the entry into Indonesia of Carrefour and Wal-Mart, who operated stores with a full range of food, clothing and household merchandise. We knew nothing about operating supermarkets, almost none of the department store skills transferred to supermarkets and we never made an appropriate ROI. Also, it turned out that neither Wal-Mart nor Carrefour were really competitors because they attracted a much more upscale customer. We had responded to a threat that did not exist, taken on all the risks of a new business and never operated the supermarket business well.

Chapter 11

Introduction to the Financial Model

Up until this point in the business concept development process, we have been focused on building a growth strategy for our business concept. Now we shift our focus to survival—determining the cash flow requirements of the new business concept—by building the financial model. **I consider this the survival step because if the new business runs out of cash, the business dies! Plan accordingly!**

The good news is that if you have properly thought through the assumptions in the five parts of the business model, it is very easy to build a proper financial model. What I have found in reviewing many, many Excel models is that entrepreneurs usually limit the detail of their assumptions to match their Excel skills. I have never found the logic of a business model assumption that cannot be captured in Excel. Improve Excel skills rather than reduce the quality of the logic in the financial model. The best Excel tutorial that I have found is from the Fuqua Business School at Duke University[ix].

I will refrain from quoting Lord Kelvin again. Math and numbers are elegant, efficient and simple to understand. The prose in a business plan may be much more challenging to understand. Build the financial model so that that a business plan is not required. **The model should be a standalone document that is completely self-explanatory.** Remember many investors now read the financial model first because it is the simplest way to understand the business concept and the business model.

Also remember that the financial model, like the business model, serves several other important purposes:

- It makes your business logic clear
- It demonstrates industry knowledge
- It clarifies the business model
- It highlights the risks (assumptions) in the business concept

Well-designed financial models make all of this information clearly apparent to the reader and also make it obvious where the weaknesses are in the business model and financial plan. Be advised!

The financial model includes nine sections:
1. *Key Assumptions*
2. *Sources and Uses*
3. *Financial Summary*
4. *Income Statement*
5. *Balance sheet*
6. *Cash Flow Statement*
7. *Capital Expenditure (CAPEX) Schedule*
8. *Headcount Schedule*
9. *Capitalization Table ("cap table")*

If the company has no non-employee shareholders, the Cap table can probably be omitted. Likewise, if CAPEX and/or headcount were not sufficiently important to include in the business model, these schedules can be omitted and replaced with some detail on the balance sheet and income statement respectively. One last note about the required sections is important. **YOU MUST INCLUDE A BALANCE SHEET!** I have noticed that Europeans frequently omit the balance sheet in financial models, relying on the cash flow statement to explain changes in the balance sheet. If you are raising money in the U.S. or from U.S. trained investors, they expect to see a balance sheet in the financial model.

A note on presentation is required at this point before explaining each of the nine sections of the financial model. I usually put the key assumptions, the sources and uses and the financial summary on one tab in the model. Why? It makes it easier for the reader to do sensitivity analysis on the assumptions and see the impact on revenue and cash flow. Building the model in a manner that makes it easy for the reviewer to use makes a difference. Difficult models get delegated to junior staff to figure out. **Easy to use models get reviewed by decision makers**. Therefore, follow my index of the nine parts of a financial model, make sensitivity analysis easy to do, and make it easy to find all the key assumptions that explain the business model.

This advice also illustrates a perhaps more fundamental point about models. A properly designed model facilitates the review of all the issues the reader is concerned about. Models are not about what the preparer thinks is important. Models should be designed to answer the important questions of the reader. The important questions to be answered are:

1. *the assumptions underlying revenue*
2. *the major areas of cost and the related gross margin and EBITDA margin; and*
3. *any other significant uses of capital.*

Do not be afraid of too much detail in any of these three areas. Sometimes it takes two hundred rows in Excel to properly explain the cost of sales for a telecom company or the revenue generated by a sales team, as shown in the chapter on CAPEX.

Lessons Learned From Indonesia

I began using an Excel-like product in 1983 or 1984 when I was shown a spreadsheet application on the Wang word processing system. It was love at first sight and I have been developing my Excel skills continuously ever since. In 1995 I went to Hong Kong to discuss with a senior executive of First Boston a bond issue for Matahari in the U.S. Early in the conversation he asked me if I knew what Matahari's annual free cash flow was. I answered the question and mentioned that we had a full financial model if he wanted to review it. He told me that he had never before had an Indonesian company interested in international financing that had a financial model. Suffice it to say we moved to the top of the priority list at First Boston and closed a $100 million bond issue six months later. The point—financial models make a difference. The world has changed since 1995 and now everybody has an Excel model of their business, but well thought out, easy to use models still make a difference to financing sources and can still move your project to the top of the list.

Chapter 12

The Parts of a Financial Model

1. Key Assumptions

Every interested investor eventually runs sensitivity analysis to determine the effects of changes in assumptions principally on revenue and cash flow. They test revenue in large part to confirm whether a market opportunity will be large enough to satisfy their ROI targets in a 5-10 year time horizon. They test cash flow to quantify the range of investment that the business will require, which is obviously a key component in determining ROI.

Given the importance of assumptions to investors, all key assumptions should be placed on a single Excel tab. There is nothing more annoying than reading through 1000 rows in a model to find a "hidden" assumption when the sensitivity analysis produces an unintuitive result.

What are the key assumptions? The key assumptions are those that explain the three key parts of the business model—growth drivers, pricing strategy and sales and distribution strategy. Now you hopefully understand why developing the business model first makes it so easy to develop a financial model. With the assumptions from the business model and a few assumptions about the four key components of working capital (accounts receivables, inventory, accounts payable and accrued expenses) most financial models are effectively built—all that is left to do is link the assumptions to the income statement, balance sheet and cash flow.

An example of the key assumptions for a website company where users can download a paid for software product is shown below. The company plans to rollout add-on products over time. The key assumptions that need to be explained are customer acquisition cost (which drives revenue), the timing of new product introductions and their acceptance rate (purchase) by the still active customers of the basic product. In this business model it is assumed that there is no "cost of sales". Most companies use a gross margin concept and this would normally be a key assumption. Gross margin and cost of sales are explained later in this chapter.

Assumptions					
Funding closing	12/31/09				
Sales/CAC					
Customer Acquisition Cost	$ 20.00				
Monthly Budget Year 1	$ 20,000	increase per month			
Budget Year 2	50.0%	of sales			
Budget after Year 2	50.0%	of sales			
% Dormant Inactive	80.0%				
Products	er Subscribe	enetration %	Year Start	Gross Mar	
Software-basic product	39.95	100%	1	0.80	
Feature Set 1	19.95	2%	7	0.90	
Feature Set 2	29.95	1%	1	0.65	
Feature Set 3	79.95	1%	2	0.40	
Feature Set 4	15.00	1%	3	0.40	
SAAS version (per month)	5.00	1%	3	0.90	
Professional version	65.00	1%	4	0.60	
Staff Additions	Active customers				
Customer Service per	15,000				
Technical Support per	15,000				
Supervisors per Cust. Serv. Ar	10				

I am often asked how many assumptions should be included in a model. I once built a model for a cellular phone distributor that had 1000 rows to explain revenue in 26 countries. Another time, a venture capitalist gave me the nicest comment on a model. He said the model was so well detailed that it saved him two weeks of due diligence (a telecom model for a company with operations in eight countries). In summary, there should be sufficient assumptions to explain thoroughly the growth driver(s) and any other major use of capital.

2. Sources and Uses

In the vernacular of finance, "sources and uses" is used instead of "cash flow statement". However, here I am using it in a slightly different way—to provide a high level summary of the capital required and the way the cash will be spent. One of the most popular posts from my blog *Sophisticated Finance* apparently discusses the concept well, and is re-printed below.

"...Now, if we were to ask what are the two or three most important questions that a business plan or financial model should answer, somewhere in the top three would probably be **"how much money do you need and for what"**. Now this question, by its nature, appears to me to be an obvious candidate for a numerical answer or an exhibit. Yet, half the business plans and models I see do not answer either question and a surprising number do not even make clear how much money they want to raise.

There is a very simple way to answer both questions in one exhibit that can be used in both a business plan and a financial model--a Sources and Uses Statement. Sources show how much you need and where it will come from and the uses show where the money is being used. All entries represent cash and cash only! The example below is a representative format and shows clearly that this company needs $3 million in new mezzanine debt and $12.2 million in new equity in order to purchase a company, buy some new equipment and provide for working capital after the acquisition.

Sources	US$		Uses	US$
Line of Credit	-		Purcshase of XX	5,500,000
Term Loan	-		Additional Equip	3,168,883
Mezzanine Debt	3,000,000		Past due AP	2,000,000
Equity for Company Ac	2,750,000		Working Capital	4,000,000
Sale of New Equity	9,418,883		Closing Costs	500,000
Total	15,168,883		Total	15,168,883

I think people leave out the "sources" because frequently they are trying to hide their lack of equity investment in the company. They leave out the "uses" probably because they have not thought through in detail what the money is for. Hiding an issue is rarely a good approach with sophisticated financiers. Use a Sources and Uses Statement in your business plan and financial model, show that you have detailed knowledge of your business and make it easier for the funding sources to understand the transaction. Lord Kelvin will be smiling down on you."

Note: the issuance of equity for the acquired company is not technically "cash" but for the sake of simplicity and understanding by the investor I included it in the Sources and Uses above. To improve understanding by investors or readers, one can break a rule.

There are two parts frequently omitted by entrepreneurs in determining the amount of capital they require. First, closing costs, which typically include the legal fees for both sides of the transaction (company and funding source). Also, include in closing costs any upfront points the bank charges for their debt. On a $90 million combination equity and mezzanine debt deal I have seen legal fees of $3 million and bank fees of $4 million. A bit on the high side but obviously significant enough to be broken out in the sources and uses. Second, working capital typically is the line where you build in a cushion for variance from plan. On a financing of $3-4 million I would add $1 million for cushion in a comparatively stable business. This would mean that if the deal closed there would be at least $1 million in undrawn lines of credit at closing, assuming there was a line of credit in the sources.

Note: I tend to ignore equity dilution when I am developing cash requirements. I am much more concerned about running out of cash, especially prematurely, than I am about giving up an additional two to five percent of equity. Typically I use 10 percent of the total capital raised as the cushion for plan variance and include that amount in working capital. The smaller the capital raise the higher percentage devoted to the working capital cushion.

3. Financial Summary

The financial summary provides key results for the company over the planning period. Key results include the key descriptors of the growth driver(s) from the business model, income statement information, working capital and debt information from the balance sheet, and closing cash position each year. A sample is shown below.

FINANCIAL SUMMARY					
USD 31-DEC	2009	2010	2011	2012	2013
Packages Sold per Year	312,000	603,745	744,081	1,184,653	1,857,012
Active Users-Cumulative	62,400	183,149	331,965	568,896	940,298
Revenue $	12,483,089	24,301,871	30,716,842	49,346,330	77,161,019
Gross Margin $	9,983,668	19,377,519	24,577,053	39,437,910	61,749,624
OPEX $	2,059,983	4,436,738	7,447,538	11,836,988	18,789,713
EBITDA $	7,923,685	14,940,782	17,129,516	27,600,922	42,959,912
Revenue Growth %	na	95%	26%	61%	56%
GM %	80%	80%	80%	80%	80%
EBITDA %	63%	61%	56%	56%	56%
Cash	6,302,517	15,976,116	26,835,817	44,219,016	71,325,055
Accounts Receivable	960,238	1,036,270	1,513,063	2,493,177	3,933,437
PP&E	93,958	165,000	215,208	290,000	405,764
Accounts Payable	506,889	657,627	983,133	1,599,399	2,528,774
Funded Debt	-	-	-	-	-
Due to Shareholders	-	-	-	-	-
Equity	7,099,824	16,769,759	27,830,955	45,652,794	73,385,483

In designing the summary there are three points to keep in mind:

1. Reinforce the business model by detailing the growth driver(s)
2. Show the operating economics in terms of margins, such as gross margin and EBITDA
3. Demonstrate the cash flow of the business and the working capital requirements

Also, do not be afraid to have a row of zeroes. For example, no debt clearly makes it obvious that the business is using equity financing or internally generated cash. No shareholder loans indicate that a new investor is not going to have to deal with this frequently troublesome issue. Good information can be shared simply by including a row of zeroes in the summary. Lastly, if there is any doubt about the currency or the units of currency ('000) make it clear in the summary.

The summary is linked to the appropriate parts of the model so that when the assumptions are tested (changed), the summary results change, making it easy for the reader to see the effects of changes (sensitivity analysis) in key assumptions for revenue and cash flow.

A point on the planning period is called for here. Personally, I always build five-year models by month. Why? Because that is the way I was taught at Chase Manhattan Bank. Secondly, five years is a very common time horizon for many investors and the tenor of many bank term loans. I do monthly results because I cannot tell you how many times I have seen seasonality create negative cash positions that do not show up on quarterly or annual projections.

If you think building a sixty period model (5 x 12) is a lot of work, you are not properly building a model. In a properly built model you develop only the first period and then you copy and paste for 59 periods. The key to being able to do this is properly developing the assumptions and knowing how to use commands such as VLOOKUP and HLOOKUP. It may take a day to properly think through how to build the assumptions, but one of the goals in designing the assumptions is to create a model where you only have to create one period. Another point related to building 60-period models should also be remembered. Build assumptions so that you can easily change the economic units. An example may illustrate the point.

A client asks you to build a model to value his 20-store retail business for a sale to a buyer. Properly done, you would model each store on its own tab so that unit economics were clear. However, this client always changes their mind, so we need to be able to include or exclude in the model any particular store based on the client's whims that day (with each store on a different tab). If you make changes for three days on individual tabs (clients never ask for just one change), by the third day nobody knows what stores are included in the model. The simpler and more understandable way to do it is to build an assumption that shows all the stores and use a zero-one switch to include or exclude each store (linking the switch to the tab for each store with VLOOKUP.) The switch is shown below.

	A	B
1		
2		
3		
4	Stores	Open-1 0-Closed
5	Adelphia	0
6	Comcast	1
7	Time Warner	0
8	Xerox	1
9		

The Vlookup command would be =Vlookup(A6,A5:B8,2) if we wanted to know whether to include the Comcast store, where A6 determines the Comcast store, A5:B8 determines the range of cells to look in and 2 says to look for the value in the second column. Names in column A need to be in alphabetical order for the formula to work properly.

After you have built a few dozen models you will realize that most of the time is spent on building the assumptions and not on the sixty periods for the income statement or cash flow. The good news is that if you use my business model methodology, the key assumptions have already been thought through ☺.

4. Income Statement

The income statement in the financial model serves three purposes.
• To document revenue growth

73

- To show the expected gross margin and EBITDA margin
- To show the path to profitability

A sample income statement is shown below. Note that the expense detail is very limited. We are not preparing this income statement to do a monthly performance review. We are providing an investor with sufficient detail to quickly understand the business. I have used this format for almost ten years and have never had an investor ask a question about operating expenses, except for salaries (which are usually detailed in a separate schedule). This level of detail also results in a comparatively small amount of "other" expense. I once saw a model with water expense broken out by department. This level of detail is what we are trying to avoid. The normal investor does not drill down to this level of expense.

Income Statement	Jan-10	Feb-10	Mar-10
Revenue			
Cost of Sales			
Gross Margin			
Operating Expenses			
Advertising & Promotion			
Auto			
Bad Debts			
Bank Service Charges			
Consultants			
Employee Benefits			
Equipment Leases			
Insurance			
Legal			
Office Rent			
Office Supplies			
Professional Fees			
Salaries			
Subscription/Membership			
Telephone			
Travel & Entertainmnet			
Other			
Total			
Operating Income			
Depreciation & Amortization			
Interest Expense			
Total			
Income Before Taxes			
Income Taxes			
Net Income			
EBITDA			

Given the importance of revenue growth, particularly to investors, we want to show a pattern to the growth in the income statement that mirrors other early stage companies without creating a "hockey stick" revenue curve. Setting aside viral success stories, growth of 100 percent per year in the early years is not uncommon. Growth then slows to the 50 percent range and normalizes at 20-25 percent in the later years. These are just rules of thumb. However, one should check the assumptions-based revenue forecast against the market opportunity requirements discussed in Appendix A. If you need a "hockey stick" forecast to satisfy investor requirements for ROI or market size, you should probably consider a different new business idea.

After revenue growth, margins are the most important financial factor in determining the attractiveness of a business concept. Gross margin (the difference between revenue and the direct costs to produce the product or service—"cost of sales") is typically evaluated by comparing it with similar companies in similar industries. To divert from industry norms typically requires a breakthrough innovation in product or service, which frankly is not likely to be the case. Low gross margins, below ten percent of sales, typically invite a great deal of scrutiny from investors and frequently lead to companies that cannot be financed. Thin gross margins put EBITDA (earnings before interest, taxes, depreciation and amortization) margins at risk, which also reduces the likelihood of good exit valuations.

EBITDA has become a very important measure in the last ten years in financial circles. EBITDA is used as a quick method to estimate a business' cash flow and is frequently used to do business valuations. It is now very common to say "I will buy your company for four times EBITDA." Another rule of thumb is that the EBITDA margin (EBITDA/Sales) should over time approach ten percent of sales. Companies with lower EBITDA margins have uncharacteristically higher cost structures (or lower gross margins), which again triggers greater investor scrutiny.

A note: investors always scrutinize the gross margin and EBITDA margin and percentages that fall outside normal ranges (particularly for a given industry) come under much greater scrutiny and reduce the likelihood of financing. SEC (Securities and Exchange Commission) filings for public companies are any easy source of information on margins (http://www.sec.gov/edgar/searchedgar/companysearch.html).

Profitability, or more precisely the path to profitability, is the third purpose served by the income statement. The path to profitability answers the question of how many years the company needs to reach a positive net income before tax. However, by now you should have realized that positive cash flow is much more important than profit. Early stage investors, such as venture capitalists, are much more concerned with seeing a company with improving performance in cash flow than a positive net income. Later stage investors, such as private equity firms, are more concerned with growth in profit (net income) and EBITDA because they typically invest in more mature companies where an IPO is the hoped for exit. Sophisticated investors usually prefer revenue growth to profitability as long as there is positive cash flow and acceptable levels of profitability.

Achieving profitability too quickly can also bring on additional investor scrutiny. The question that will be asked is--can you grow revenue faster if we postpone profitability? Aside from the obvious benefits achieved from growth such as economies of scale, market share, etc., there is an additional benefit. Many early stage companies raise multiple rounds of capital before reaching profitability or positive cash flow. How do you value such companies? One method investors use is to take the last valuation of the company and multiply it by [1+compounded growth rate of revenue] since the last valuation. A simple illustration is below.

Valuation	31-Mar-07	$12,500,000
CAGR Revenue thru	31-Mar-10	37.80%
Valuation	31-Mar-10	$17,225,000

Note: CAGR-compounded annual growth rate

I saw this technique used before the economic crisis in 2008. Given that valuations have declined by about forty percent since then, this technique may no longer be so common. However, the technique illustrates another reason to accelerate revenue growth—it may help valuation in subsequent rounds of capital raising.

A Note on Expense Assumptions: Most of the key expense assumptions were developed when the business model was prepared and include staffing and customer acquisition cost. While some investors praise models with very detailed expenses in the income statement, my experience is that investors only show interest in important expenses related to the growth driver(s). Expenses related to product development may be sufficiently significant to justify their own schedule detailing the assumptions, but the summary of this cost is added as a line in the income statement.

5. Balance Sheet

Most sophisticated readers of financial statements start with the balance sheet, as evidenced in part by the fact that every audited statement prepared by a CPA begins with the balance sheet. The balance sheet serves several purposes.

- It details the working capital position of the company and the various components of working capital (a use of cash)
- It details any other significant investment in assets (a use of cash)
- It illustrates the capital structure of the company which includes borrowed money and equity investment (a source of cash)

Therefore, in building the balance sheet in the financial model a key objective is to bring clarity and understanding to each of these three issues. A sample balance sheet is shown below with highlights for each of the three issues.

Assets		Liabilities & Shareholders Equity		
Current Assets		**Current Liabilities**		
Cash	275	Line of Credit		Working Capital
Accounts Receivable	628	CPLTD		
Inventory	-	Accounts Payable	180	Other Significant Asset
Prepaid Expenses		Accrued Expenses		
Total Current Assets	903	Income Taxes Payable		Capital Structure
		Total Current Liabilities	180	
Property, Plant & Equipment				
Property		**Long Term Liabilities**		
Plant & Equipment		Long Term Debt		
Accumulated Depreciation		Due to Shareholders		
Net PP&E		Total Long Term Liabilities		
		Total Liabilities		
Other Assets				
		Stockholders' Equity / (Deficit):		
Total Assets	1,129	Common Stock		
		Preferred Series A		
		Preferred Series B & D		
		Additional Paid in Capital		
		Retained Earnings/(Deficit)		
		Net Income / (Loss)		
		Total Stockholders' Equity / (Deficit)		
		Total Liabilities and Stockholders' Equity / (Deficit)	1,129	
		Check Total	0	

Working capital (current assets minus current liabilities) assumptions are probably the only assumptions required to forecast a balance sheet that were not part of preparing the business model. I recommend that a days on hand (DOH) technique be used to forecast the four parts of working capital—accounts receivables, inventory, accounts payable and accrued expenses. For example, accounts receivables is calculated using monthly days on hand as follows.

Current month sales x 12/ (target DOH AR/360)= value of AR current month

Target DOH is the expected number of days of sales you expect to have in accounts receivable at any month end and should approximate the expected credit terms given to customers or received from suppliers. To determine the balance sheet values for inventory and accounts payable substitute current month cost of sales (revenue-gross margin) instead of current month sales in the formula above. For accrued expenses I normally assume half of the current month SG&A value. In a highly seasonal business where inventory is ordered well in advance you may want to substitute a future month cost of sales instead of the current month in order to start building inventory to properly capture the working capital requirements.

The second part of the assets side of the balance sheet is to develop the capital expenditure requirements (CAPEX) and the resultant plant, property and equipment. Of course, first let me say, that you will have no property (real estate) on the balance sheet. If an investor wanted a portfolio of real estate and early stage investments they would create it themselves and need no help from a fledgling entrepreneur who foolishly invests in real estate.

In businesses that have a significant investment in plant and equipment, such as telecom, retail, restaurants, steel making, etc., you would have developed the detailed assumptions about CAPEX as part of the business model in order to understand unit economics or to explain the physical delivery of a service (e.g. telecom). So, to create the CAPEX in the financial model, one merely uses the business model assumptions.

The last part of the asset side of the balance sheet deals with other assets, which usually has no entries for most startups. One might include customer deposit cash, a patent or a license paid for but only if they are significant dollar values, say greater than $250,000. Any other asset probably has no effect on cash flow and can be ignored, (e.g. prepaid expenses). Remember the financial model is not an accounting examination.

Now we move to the right hand side of the balance sheet. Given that current liabilities were covered in the discussion of working capital above, we only need to deal with the capital structure. Capital structure includes borrowed money and equity. One could also include leases but why over complicate by including them. I have never seen a financing where the investor or banker scrutinized leases payable. Also, if you fail to secure the lease financing, you have probably understated the capital required in the capital raise.

Borrowed money falls into four categories.
- Short term senior bank debt (includes loan sharks and any other short term notes)
- Senior bank term loans (>1 year tenor)
- Subordinated debt (also called mezzanine debt)

- Convertible debentures (loans with an option to convert to equity under specified conditions)

Subordinated loans are loans where in the event of bankruptcy the senior debt receives liquidation proceeds before subordinated loan holders. Subordinated debt provides additional cushion to senior lenders (in the same way as equity) and is an alternative to equity. However, in contrast to equity, mezzanine lenders look to the existing cash flow for repayment more so than forecasted performance. Typically subordinated debt equals 1x EBITDA and senior debt equals 3X EBITDA. Therefore, total borrowed money equals 4x EBITDA. If you are KKR or Blackstone, premier private equity firms, you can leverage more than 4x, but if you work for these firms you probably skipped this chapter on financial model building.

Convertible debentures can be either senior debt or subordinated debt, but they always have an equity conversion feature and are typically a mandatory conversion at the time of an IPO (initial public offering). Whether you should choose senior or subordinated convertible brings up an important point. Always fill in your capital structure from the bottom up. In other words first arrange equity, then subordinated debt and then senior debt, if possible. Financing sources rarely want to be subordinated to previous lenders. Also, the most stable funding sources with the least onerous repayment terms are usually at the bottom of the capital structure. Yes, these sources have higher risk and therefore need a higher return, but securing capital and a stable capital structure is much more important than the cost of money. If you have an uncontrollable urge to negotiate fiercely loan rates become a mortgage broker and forego entrepreneurship.

Each of the four types of borrowed money and loans from shareholders should be detailed in the financial model. Remember zeroes convey information.

Some people use short-term bank debt as the value to balance the cash flow. They opt for this approach because they want cash to always have a fixed value. In other words, if you think you always need to have $6 million in cash on hand to run the business, this value becomes a constant on the balance sheet and short-term debt becomes the value to balance the cash flow. The problem with this method is that if an investor is sensitizing assumptions to see the effect on cash flow, the cash does not change with the assumptions. Therefore, the investor has to invest the time to rebuild the model, which is not very user friendly and to be avoided. I prefer an alternative approach that some people call the self-balancing model.

The self-balancing model works as follows. Build the entire balance sheet in the financial model except for the cash row. Then prepare the cash flow. Link the ending cash balance from the cash flow to the cash row in the balance sheet. If you did the cash flow properly, the ending cash position on the cash flow statement provides a value for cash on the balance sheet such that total assets equal total liabilities plus shareholders equity.

(Note: financial models where total assets do not equal total liabilities plus shareholders equity get thrown in the wastebasket usually. Nobody has the time to teach basic accounting.)

The equity structure on the balance sheet includes four parts.
- Investment in preferred stock (receives liquidation proceeds before common stock holders)

- Investment in common stock (the total value; ignore paid-in-capital)
- Retained earnings
- Period net income (usually monthly or annual depending on the timeframe used in the model)

Many sophisticated investors invest using preferred stock or convertible debentures. Therefore, one should probably detail each round of common and preferred stock on the balance sheet to make it clear that the company probably has a complex equity structure that requires more investor due diligence. Showing issues upfront is almost always the best policy. Surprises late in a deal, such as three rounds of different preferred stock, have a tendency to kill deals (you look like an amateur).

If you do not understand retained earnings and the net income for the period, you lack sufficient knowledge of accounting to build a financial model. Your knowledge of accounting may be sufficient to prepare a financial model when you understand the expression "retained earnings rolls forward". Sorry, but basic accounting is generally outside the scope of this book. A good introductory accounting text is Fundamentals of Financial Accounting by Glenn A. Welsch and Daniel G. Short.

6. Cash Flow Statement

The cash flow statement is designed to highlight the sources and uses of cash, or the inflows and outflows of cash. The cash flow statement is important for several reasons:
- It highlights the cash used to support working capital, an area of keen interest to most investors

- It highlights changes in the capital structure, such as the risk associated with adding debt or planned future equity issuances which may be dilutive
- It forms the basis for a company valuation, which in one of many possible forms (discounted cash flow, EBITDA multiples, etc.) is always based on cash flow or potential cash flow

I am not going to explain in detail how to prepare a cash flow. You were supposed to learn that in introductory accounting. Simply put, increases in assets are a use of cash and increases in liabilities are a source of cash. Add the net effect of these changes to the opening cash position to arrive at the ending cash position. The ending cash position determined should be such that the total assets equal the total liabilities plus shareholder equity on the balance sheet.

An example of a standard cash flow and the related income statement and balance sheet is available on Sophisticated Finance[x]. This cash flow also illustrates an important point in preparing a cash flow statement, non-cash items in the income statement are added back to cash flow (remember cash flow statements reflect only changes in cash). All the links between the income statement, balance sheet and cash flow statement should help those with limited experience in preparing a cash flow.

7. Cap Table

The cap table, short hand for the capitalization table, shows the equity investment in the company on a fully diluted basis. Therefore, it would show the preferred shares and common stock issued, preferably by series (each issuance at a different price). For each issuance of preferred or common stock, any warrants or options granted and the fully diluted number of shares of common stock they convert into is also shown. A representative example of a cap table is shown below.

Shareholders	Pre-Deal Capitalization Structure						
	Common Stock	Options & Restricted Stock	Series A Preferred	Series B Preferred	Series C Preferred	Common Stock Warrants	Total
Chico	2,782,887	6,693,750	.	.	.	6,527,756	16,004,393
Groucho	681,875	.	.	.	.	.	681,875
Harpo	1,591,622	.	.	.	.	.	1,591,622
Zeppo	987,188	.	209,110	.	.	.	1,196,298
Other Investors / Employees	4,280,030	513,500	496,218	.	.	.	5,289,748
Investor 1	.	.	11,064	39,560,616	21,686,947	9,400,242	70,658,869
Investor 2	956,833	.	.	.	48,193,215	37,882,382	87,032,430
Unallocated Option Pool	.	372,500	.	.	.	.	372,500
Total	11,280,435	7,579,750	716,392	39,560,616	69,880,162	53,810,380	182,827,735

Note: My apologies to the Marx brothers for using them to represent the employee shareholders.

Cap tables come in for a great deal of scrutiny in investor due diligence because investors want to be sure they are getting the percentage of the company they think they are buying. It is recommended that a company keep its cap table current. Reconstructing a cap table can be a long, expensive process when there have been several equity issuances.

8. Conclusions

In preparing a financial model there are a few important tips to keep in mind.

- The model should be self-explanatory and require no walk through with the preparer to explain the logic of the model layout or design
- The model should follow the accounting principles of GAAP (generally accepted accounting principles; used in the U.S.) or IFRS (international

financial reporting standards; used in the rest of the world and soon to be adopted in the U.S.)

- Detail should be developed to explain the "business model" and should be minimized in non-important areas
- Assumptions should be highlighted (typically in bold blue) in order to make them obvious and facilitate sensitivity analysis
- Any assumption based on logic can be captured in Excel, if you have developed sufficient Excel skills

Lessons Learned From Indonesia

While venture capitalists generally structure their investments through preferred stock, my time in Asia suggests that billionaires who are investing their own money prefer convertible bonds. I did two or three investments with a company controlled by a well-known Asian tycoon and heard about several more and in every case the investment instrument of choice was convertible debt.

Convertible debt is a debt instrument with an option to convert the loan balance to equity at a conversion price agreed at loan signing. Why was this instrument so popular with Asian tycoons? The reasons are:

1. It provided current income through interest payments
2. It matched the risk of the investment; equity-like risk should earn equity returns
3. It provided for a means to recover the capital through loan repayment if the equity option never appreciated, thus tending to better safeguard the investor capital

The interest payments are at below market rates because of the value of the equity option, thus putting less strain on cash flow. The conversion price for the equity is generally above any then current market price for the common stock, which reduces the dilutive effect at conversion.

In companies with a strong growth story, I prefer convertible debt to common or preferred stock as the investment instrument. I rarely saw the equity option priced correctly in a convertible instrument even by allegedly sophisticated investors. Thus, I was able to raise equity at better than market prices. For more on equity option pricing, study the Black Scholes formula.

Chapter 13
Practical Application of the Business Model

In 2007 when I started blogging on Sophisticated Finance I did a facetious post about the "Hacker Universal Theory of Management (HUTM)" in which I argued that the management of a business could be greatly simplified by just focusing on the growth driver(s) in the business. In a subsequent blog post I talked about a speaking tour sponsored by the Hooters restaurant chain to promote HUTM and the need for a book to sell on the speaking tour. While I consider this my funniest blog post ever, over the subsequent years in thinking about business model, I have come to realize that managing the business by focusing on the growth drivers is a sound and understandable management approach and would help entrepreneurs to focus on what is important.

Most entrepreneurs are usually good at some of the following:

- *product development and/or technology*
- *selling the product*
- *story telling to raise capital or entice new employees*

Most entrepreneurs initially have little experience in:

- *business strategy*
- *managing an organization*
- *cash flow management*
- *raising capital*

This last chapter in the book discusses how to use the concept of the business model and the related financial model to overcome the inexperience of most entrepreneurs.

Business Strategy

Business strategy is fundamentally an allocation of resources problem. The resources to be allocated are capital, people and management time. The objective is to increase shareholder wealth, which requires growing cash flow, and to do this in an economically efficient way (otherwise known as generating an appropriate rate of return). In summary, business strategy is the allocation of resources to increase shareholder wealth in an economically efficient way. Where most entrepreneurs have trouble is in allocating their limited resources appropriately, which leads to no increase in shareholder wealth or "sub par" returns for investors.

As you may recall from the Preface, the entrepreneur's first objective is revenue growth, followed by positive cash flow and then profitability. The business model makes it quite clear where resources should be allocated. All three resources-- people, capital and management time--should typically be focused on one of the five growth drivers and the supporting sales and distribution strategy. (Ignore everything else, with the possible exception of a management information system to track the performance of the growth drivers.) **In early stage companies, if it does not involve the growth driver, ignore it or outsource it.**

Some might argue that new product iterations are critical in a startup and the focus on the growth driver alone is wrong. I believe that approaching the problem from the perspective of the growth driver brings you closer to the customer than focusing on product features. For example, no amount of new features will help a social media site if you cannot first master search engine optimization (SEO) or other techniques that bring potential subscribers to the website. Therefore, the company should first master SEO or viral marketing before it invests more time and money in new product features. (SEO and viral marketing are two types of customer acquisition expense frequently seen when the growth driver is subscribers and the industry sector is social media).

Managing an Organization

Entrepreneurs inherently have a problem with focus and frequently micromanage every task in their startup. A simple rule to consider is "if the decision will not put you out of business, ignore it or delegate it". Now with your time management skills greatly improved, you can focus your time on the growth drivers and sales strategy and eventually distribution strategy.

Given the scarcity of resources in a startup, outsource any activity that does not affect the growth driver in the business. This approach will not only free up capital to invest in the growth driver but also will eliminate the need to devote substantial management time to unimportant tasks. I once ran a high tech company doing $300 million in revenue per year with nine people on payroll and everybody was involved in sales except two accounting people and one supply chain management executive. If you have the discipline to look for outsourcing from the beginning, management can be simplified to focusing only on revenue and the growth driver. Another advantage to outsourcing is that fixed costs are lower, management decisions are simplified by almost every decision being based on marginal costs and variable costs are easier to manage especially in a downturn,

Current management theory advocates running a business based on the key performance indicators (KPI). KPIs are the most important operating statistics that show the health of the business and its trends. Despite the popularity of KPIs little useful information is available to help an entrepreneur determine the KPIs for a business. Using the business model methodology makes it easy to develop the KPIs. Each key assumption that explains the growth driver is a KPI. Remember we said that the assumptions for the growth drivers make clear the risks in the business model. The risks in the business model are where we should focus management attention. Now, hopefully it is obvious that the risks in the business model are the key performance indicators.

Cash Flow Management

I have said repeatedly that running out of cash puts the company out of business. If you have developed a business model and extended it to a monthly financial model, then it becomes quite easy to forecast future cash flows. In a simple example, if you update the model for the month's actual results by replacing the forecasted month, you immediately have a forecast of the future cash position. In a slightly more sophisticated approach you could update the sales forecast and operating expenses for future months based on the actual month's results. As soon as the model shows negative cash or near negative cash you know you need to think about a capital raise or drastically changing the operating economics of the business. Hint: it is probably more prudent to raise new capital.

One important point to remember is to update the balance sheet in the model for the actual ending values of the month. Working capital problems put more people out of business than income statement problems. If days on hand for the four components of working capital have changed, these assumptions in the model need to change.

Raising Capital

A common mistake by entrepreneurs is to assume they can raise additional capital faster than actual market conditions permit. I always assume I need a year to raise new money from banks or investors, even in good times. Therefore, as soon as you see a forecast of negative cash or a near negative cash position, one should start organizing a capital raise. If you have kept the model updated for actual results every month, then one of the most time consuming activities—building the forecasted model—is already done.

If the company is experiencing very high growth, 100 percent or more, I would probably like to raise capital 2-3 years in advance. If growth is stronger than expected, one does not want to slow the company down waiting to complete a capital raise. A more conservative two-year time horizon is also attractive in emerging markets where capital availability is more volatile. In highly uncertain times I have seen leading international banks cancel or reduce bank lines in emerging markets. Therefore, in your two year planning horizon, one should not be highly reliant on lines of credit. Lines of credit are cheaper than term loans or equity but they tend to disappear in tough economic conditions when you especially need them.

Most entrepreneurs do not raise capital frequently and therefore do not have a lot of experience in doing it, have limited knowledge of alternative financing structures and little idea of market pricing or terms. Therefore, for anything but the simplest bank line, one should hire a financial advisor. (The one exception would be a venture-backed company where the VCs typically are very good at capital raising.) In hiring an advisor, industry expertise, experience in all types of financing, completed financings and reputation are the four key factors in selection. Be wary of advisors that charge six figure fees upfront unless you are considering a top tier Wall Street firm. Large upfront fees are typically a warning sign that should not be ignored.

Entrepreneurs love to negotiate fees, interest rates and valuation. These negotiations are very time consuming, de-motivate the bankers and capital sources and rarely improve the entrepreneur's position. If you have well grounded knowledge of market terms, do not negotiate much when terms are at or near market.

The logic for this perhaps counter-intuitive position is as follows:
1. *Your time is more valuable managing the business.*
2. *The longer the process of capital raising the greater the likelihood that the company could have bad results in a quarter and turn off the investor*
3. *During long negotiations market conditions could change adversely and prevent the capital raise*

I once priced a five-year bond issue on the day when the T-bill rate was at a ten year high. Two years later the capital markets completely closed down in Asia and the $100 million five-year bond that I had obtained looked very, very cheap. Always take the money when you can and do not worry so much about the cost. Certainty of cash is invaluable, especially in high growth scenarios and in volatile market conditions.

Conclusion

In conclusion:

1. *Do not run out of cash*
2. *Raise cash early*
3. *Do not spend a lot of time negotiating better terms, if the terms offered are near market*
4. *Focus on the growth driver*
5. *Manage the KPIs because they represent the risks in the business model*

One additional thought in closing. I have not talked about getting rich in this book. The three billionaires I worked for never talked about their wealth. Building a large company is about creating something special which hopefully makes the world a better place. To quote a blog post by Eric Ries, Venture Advisor at Kleiner Perkins:

> "Every startup has a chance to change the world, by bringing not just a new product, but an entirely new institution into existence. That institution will touch many people in its life: customers, investors, employees, and everyone they touch as well. I believe we have an obligation to ensure the resulting impact is worthy of the energies we invest in bringing it to life."

This very elegant thought is what business is really about. This is the last and most important lesson from Indonesia. Hopefully I have given the reader some tools to reach this lofty goal.

APPENDIX A
How Big is the Market Opportunity

How big is the market for a business concept is really a question that cannot be answered. I find that most investors actually ask "Is the market large enough to justify the investment requested? How do investors make a determination of whether a market opportunity is large enough to justify the requested invested. One technique I have seen used, which involves a bit of math, is shown below.

$I \times R = S \times E \times X \times P$

I- Amount of investment by investor

R-Multiple of investment to be returned

S- Sales in the year of exit

E-EBITDA margin as percent of sales

X- exit multiple of EBITDA

P- Percent of company the investor owns

Solving for S, sales in the year of exit, gives us

$S = I \times R / (E \times X \times P)$

An example will make it all clear and show how useful this little tool is.

An investor invests $4 million in return for a 40 percent shareholding in a company and expects to get back 10 times his money in year five, a standard return model for VCs. The investor assumes that the exit (sale of the company) will be at 8 times EBITDA in year five, a reasonable assumption before the economic crisis in 2008. This company is in an industry where EBITDA margins are 15 percent, so the investor assumes the company will have this margin.

Plugging in these values in the formula above shows the following result.

$S = \$4\text{million} \times 10 / (.15 \times 8 \times .40) = \$83.33$ million

The investors need to have confidence that the company can reach sales of $83 million in year five in order to generate their 10 X return on the investment of $4 million. Assessing the reasonableness of $83 million in sales in year 5 is much more manageable than the open-ended question—how big is the market? If the company projections showed Year 5 sales of $60 million, the investment opportunity would most likely be declined.

One should also note that capital efficiency (I) and operating margins (E) have a dramatic effect on the Year 5 sales required. In the example above, if I equals only $2 million and E equals 30 percent, Year 5 sales need only reach $20.83 million. These results make clear the importance of capital efficiency and the constant effort to improve operating margins. Obviously, lower capital requirements and higher EBITDA margins make an investment opportunity more attractive.

APPENDIX B

Industry Growth Drivers

Shown below are the typical growth drivers for a variety of industries.

Industry	Growth Driver
Agricultural production	Distribution
Auto sales	New Locations
Chemicals	Accounts
Construction equipment	Distribution
Electronic equipment	Supplies-accounts; enduser-distribution
Financial services	Sales force
Food manufacturing	Distribution
Furniture	Distribution
Hotels	New Locations
Marine transportation	Accounts
Metal production	Supplies-accounts; enduser-distribution
Mining	Accounts
Newspapers	Sales force (advertising)
Oil & gas production	Distribution
Paper products	Supplies-accounts; enduser-distribution
Professional services	Sales force
Railroads	New Locations (stations)
Real estate development	Sales force
Restaurants	New Locations
Retail	New Locations
Textile manufacturing	Accounts
Tires & automotive parts	Supplies-accounts; enduser-distribution
Transportation services	Sales force
Trucking	Accounts
Utilities	Subscribers
Wholesale distribution	Accounts

APPENDIX C

Pricing Strategy Definitions

The pricing strategy alternatives and their definitions are shown below.

Immediate	Deferred	Indirect
$/Unit	Free trials	Advertising
BOGO (Buy 1, Give Another)	Freemium	Barter
Donations	Lease	
Rentals	Intervals (Time Share)	
Commissions	Service/Maintenance fees	
	Licensing (I.P.)	
	Additional services	
	Membership/subscription	

$/Unit—the traditional purchase paid in cash at time of purchase

BOGO—the customer purchases two units; one is for customer use and the second unit is donated to a charitable purpose (made famous by One Laptop Per child[xi])

Donations—the compensation, if any, to the product or service provider is determined at the sole discretion of the customer; compensation may be directed to a third party such as a charity at the request of the provider

Rentals—limited time use of a product or service in return for a cash payment at the time of use

Commissions—In return for the use of a product or service, a third party pays the provider

Free trials—the customer can use the product or service for free for a limited time, after which they must pay to continue using

Freemium—the customer can use the product or service for free, but the expectation is that a certain percentage of customers will purchase a version of the product with a larger, richer feature set

Lease— extended time use of a product or service in return for cash payments over the lease period; ownership of the product or service may or may not be with the customer

Intervals (time share)—Multiple customers have the right to use a product or service usually in return for a one-time initial payment

Service/Maintenance Fees—Principal compensation to the provider comes from annual payments rather than an initial payment for the goods or service

Licensing—the right to use a product rather than purchase it, with many different payment schemes used

Additional Services—the product or service is given away (or a nominal initial payment) but to realize the full benefits additional cash payments are required for additional features or services (sometimes referred to as "bate and switch")

Membership/Subscription—the customer needs to pay to belong to an organization, in return for which they receive certain benefits

Advertising—the customer receives a service during which they are exposed to a third parties advertising; the placement of the advertising compensates the provider (the "Google Model")

Barter—Goods or services are exchanged for other goods and services from a third party; such goods are eventually sold for cash or used by the provider to realize the economic benefit

Footnotes

[i] U.S. Department of Labor

[ii] (http://www.presentationzen.com/presentationzen/2009/08/10-tips-on-how-to-think-like-a-designer.html)

[iii] http://designmind.frogdesign.com/blog/escaping-commoditization-and-today039s-other-common-business-challenges.html?utm_source=feedburner&utm_medium=feed&utm_campaign=Feed%3A+frog-design-mind+%28design+mind%29&utm_content=Google+Reader

[iv] http://www.mckinseyquarterly.com/Cultivating_innovation_an_interview_with_the_CEO_of_a_leading_Italian_design_firm_2299.

[v] Zaltman, G. 2008. Marketing Metaphoria: What Deep Metaphors Reveal About the Minds of Consumers. Boston. Harvard Business Press

[vi] http://www.isc.hbs.edu/

[vii] Alexanderson, G. 2002. *The Random Walks of George Polya.* Washington. The Mathematical Association of America

[viii] This concept was derived from the collective work of Professor Rita Gunther McGrath http://ritamcgrath.com/blog/

[ix] http://faculty.fuqua.duke.edu/~pecklund/ExcelReview/ExcelReview.htm

[x] http://sophisticatedfinance.typepad.com/sophisticated_finance/2008/02/startup-excel-m.html

[xi] One Laptop Per Child http://laptop.org